I0753259

TAINTOR'S
ROUTE AND CITY GUIDES
CITY OF
NEW YORK
TAINTOR BROTHERS & CO.,
758 Broadway, New York.

THE

CITY OF NEW YORK.

A Complete Guide,

WITH

DESCRIPTIVE SKETCHES OF OBJECTS AND PLACES OF INTEREST, AND CONDENSED TABLES OF CHURCHES, INSTITUTIONS, BANKS, HOTELS, CITY RAILROADS, FERRIES, STAGE LINES, AMUSEMENTS, ETC. ALSO TRAVELER'S DIRECTORY FOR RAILROADS, STEAMBOATS, OCEAN STEAMERS;

AND A

COMPLETE NEW STREET DIRECTORY

ILLUSTRATED WITH MAP AND WOODCUTS.

NEW YORK:
TAINTOR BROTHERS & CO.,
758 BROADWAY.
1876.

INDEX.

Amusements........................ 39
Approaches........................ 9
Art Galleries........................ 42
Avenues, Other........................ 39
Banks........................ 67
Battery........................ 14
Bowery........................ 31
Bowling Green........................ 15
Broadway........................ 14
Bridle Road........................ 47
Carriage Fares........................ 70
Carousal........................ 48
Casino........................ 50
Cave........................ 51
Cemeteries........................ 54
Central Park........................ 46
Central Park, Afoot........................ 47
Central Park Directory........................ 45
Charitable Institutions........................ 63
Churches........................ 56
Christian Associations........................ 62
City Hall........................ 19
City Hall Park........................ 19
City Railroads........................ 70
Clubs........................ 66
Colleges and Seminaries........................ 63
Commons........................ 49
Courts........................ 69
Court House........................ 19
Dairy........................ 48
Distances in the City........................ 69
Eighth Avenue........................ 38
Excursions Round About........................ 53
Ferries........................ 73
Fourth Avenue and Bowery........................ 31
Grand Central Depot........................ 34
Great Circle........................ 49
Hack Fares........................ 70
Historical Sketch........................ 11
Hotels........................ 65
Lexington Avenue........................ 30
Location........................ 7
Libraries........................ 43
Lake........................ 50
Location of Piers........................ 74
Mall........................ 48
Madison Avenue........................ 29
Madison Square........................ 25
Marble Arch........................ 48
Markets........................ 69
Museum and Menagerie........................ 49
Park Avenue........................ 31
Parks, Other........................ 52
Play Ground........................ 48
Police Stations........................ 68
Post Office........................ 18
Railroads........................ 75
Ramble........................ 50
Safe Deposit Companies........................ 68
Schiller Monument........................ 51
Seventh Avenue........................ 38
Sixth Avenue........................ 36
Springs........................ 52
Stage Routes........................ 69
St. Paul's Church........................ 17
Steamboats, Coastwise and River........................ 76
Steamers, Ocean........................ 82
Street Directory........................ 85
Street System........................ 12
Terrace........................ 50
Third Avenue........................ 36
Topography........................ 7
Travelers' Directory........................ 75
Trinity Church........................ 16
Trust Company........................ 68
Union Square........................ 23

CITY OF NEW YORK.

Its Location and Topography.

NEW YORK, the chief city of the United States and the Western Continent, is located at the mouth of the Hudson River, in the southern part of the State of New York. The City Hall is in latitude 40°42′43″ N., longitude 74°0′3″ W., and the city occupies the county of the same name. It covers the whole of Manhattan Island and a portion of the mainland, and is bounded on the south by New York Bay; on the west by the Hudson or North River; on the north by the city of Yonkers and Westchester County, N.Y.; on the east by the river Bronx, that separates it from Westchester County, and the East River, a narrow, salt-water strait, dividing it from Long Island. It also includes Randall's, Ward's, and Blackwell's Islands, in the East River; and Governor's Island, occupied by the U. S. Government; Bedloe's and Ellis' Islands, in the Bay. Spuyten Duyvil Creek and Harlem River divide the city into two unequal portions, and make the northern boundary of Manhattan Island. The city is 16 miles long, and varies in width from a few hundred yards to 4¼ miles at the north part. Its area is about 41½ square miles, or 26,500 acres, of which 12,100 are on the mainland. Its location is both beautiful, healthful, and advantageous in a commercial sense. Its commodious bay, the Hudson River, the neighboring sea, and the diversified country about it, contribute to its attractiveness, while its varied surface and extensive water front conduce to its general healthfulness. Its harbor gives ample and safe anchorage for large fleets, and opens directly upon the Atlantic. Its position in the center of the northern part of the coast makes it a natural entrépot for the Middle States; and the Hudson River, navigable for nearly 150 miles, places it in easy communication with the interior. The Erie Canal and several lines of railroads place the city in reach of the Great West, and on the east, New England almost joins the city. The State and City of New Jersey fringe the opposite bank of the Hudson, and along the East River the city of Brooklyn and its neighboring towns form a continuous city upon its eastern side. From the Battery, at the southern end of Manhattan Island, the view of the Bay,

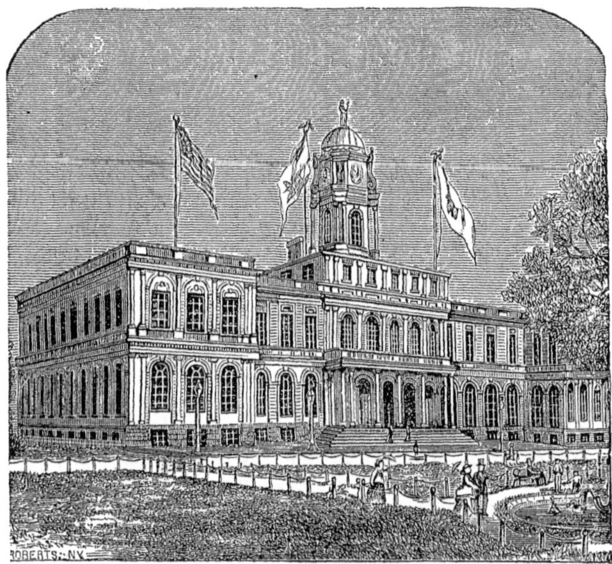

CITY HALL.

the Islands, Brooklyn Heights, Staten Island, the Jersey shore, Jersey City, and the entrance to the Hudson, presents one of the most animated and beautiful pictures to be found. The upper part of the city lies opposite the Palisades, and is remarkable for its rural and picturesque scenery. Its topography is at once favorable for business purposes and good drainage. The lower part of Manhattan Island, from the Battery north for about 3½ miles, is rolling and sandy in character. It then rises slightly and becomes very rocky. At Central Park, near the center of the city, it rises into broken hills; and northward, along the river, the land rises to a height of 238 feet at Washington Heights. Above the Island the land is hilly and rough, with a great variety of scenery. The lower part of the city has been much altered by filling and grading, and the original width has been materially increased by filling in the rivers on both sides. The city is compactly built up to 59th Street, at the southern end of Central Park; and on the east of the Park it extends some 3½ miles farther to the Harlem River. This location is sometimes known as Harlem and Yorkville, being the sites of those villages. West of Central Park the population centers in the villages of Bloomingdale and Manhattanville. North of these, along the Hudson, are Washington Heights, Inwood, Kingsbridge, Spuyten Duyvil, Mosholu, Riverdale, and Mount St. Vincent. North of Harlem River are Mott Haven, Morrisania, West Farms, North New York, Port Morris, Woodstock, Highbridgeville, Claremont, Tremont, Mount Hope, Mount Eden, Fairmount, Belmont, Fordham, and Williamsbridge. All of these places are now included in New York City, and, as the city is rapidly spreading, it promises to be one of the largest and most populous in the world.

The Ways of Approach

to New York are numerous, since it is in communication with all parts of the globe, either by sea or railroad. From the sea it is approached from the south by Sandy Hook through the Narrows, between Long Island on the east, and Staten Island on the west, into New York Bay, passing the great fortresses of Fort Tompkins and Fort Richmond on the west, or Staten Island shore, and Fort Hamilton on the east, or Long Island shore, while old Fort Lafayette, of the "Great Rebellion" celebrity, stands in the bay, a short distance from the shore. At the confluence of the East and Hudson Rivers is Governor's Island, distinguished by the circular fortress on its northern shore. The Cunard line of steamers lands its passengers at Jersey City; the Hamburg and German lines at Hoboken; while the Inman, White Star, Anchor, National and French lines, discharge theirs at different piers on the Hudson River, or west side of the city. There is another channel of approach from the sea through the Kills, between Staten

Island, on the New Jersey shore, connecting Raritan Bay with New York Harbor—but only vessels of light draught approach by this route.

Steamers and vessels approaching from Long Island Sound pass through Hell Gate and discharge cargoes on both the East River and North River piers. The Hartford, New Haven, Bridgeport, and other steamboats from nearer ports, land at East

BROADWAY, CORNER BARCLAY STREET.

River piers—at Peck Slip and vicinity; while the Fall River, Stonington, Providence, Norwich and New London, and Boston outside lines, pass round the Battery and discharge at North or Hudson River piers. The Hudson River steamboats all discharge on the west or North River side of the city. Passengers via New York and New Haven, Harlem, New York Central and Hudson River Railroads, are dropped at the Grand Central Depot, East 42d street and Fourth Avenue. All railroad passengers from Boston and the East are landed at Grand Central Depot. The Pennsylvania Railroad lands its passengers by ferry-boat, from Jersey City, at Cortlandt street and Desbrosses street. The Erie

Railroad, Northern New Jersey and Midland Railroads by ferry to Chambers street and West 23d street. Central New Jersey by ferry to Liberty street. Delaware, Lackawanna and Western by ferry to Barclay and Christopher streets. New Jersey Southern by ferry to Murray street. Staten Island by ferry to Whitehall, and Long Island by ferry to Roosevelt and E. 34th streets.

Historical Sketch.

Jean Verrazani, a Florentine navigator, entered the Bay of New York in 1525, but, his explorations being interrupted by a sudden storm, put to sea without making a permanent settlement.

Manhattan Island was first visited by Europeans in September, 1609, when Henry Hudson in his yacht, "The Half Moon," entered the bay and sailed up the river. The information he carried back to Holland led to repeated visits by Dutch traders, and in 1624 a formal settlement was made. In 1826, under Peter Minnet, Fort Amsterdam was built, and the entire island was purchased of the Indians for $24, paid in goods. In 1664 the place was taken under English control, and the name was changed from New Amsterdam to New York. In 1673 it was retaken by the Dutch, but their occupancy was short, and it soon reverted to the English. From 1674 it began to grow rapidly, and at the time of the Revolution was a city of 23,000 inhabitants. In the Revolution it took an early and active part till captured by the British in 1776. It was occupied by them till 1783, when it was finally evacuated at the close of the war. From 1785 to 1790 New York was the seat of Government of the United States, President Washington having been inaugurated in the old City Hall, then located at the corner of Nassau and Wall streets. The free school system was founded in 1805, and in 1807 the Hudson was first navigated with steamboats by Robert Fulton. The present system of streets north of Houston street was planned in 1821, and the survey occupied ten years. The first steam ferry was opened in 1814, and in 1817 the first line of packets sailed for Liverpool. Gas was introduced in 1825 and the Croton water in 1842. Several great fires have impeded the growth of the city, but it has continually advanced northward, and seems, in time, destined to cover its entire area with stores and houses. The original charter of the city was granted by James II., of England, in 1686. Another was granted by George II., in 1730. This

Old Post Office.

charter was of the most liberal character, and made New York practically a free city, and was the law till 1829, when a new charter was made by the people. This charter, with its various amendments, formed the basis of the present law of the city. The following table illustrates the growth of the city in population:

Year	Population	Year	Population
1653	1,120	1820	123,706
1661	1,743	1825	166,136
1675	2,580	1830	202,589
1696	4,455	1835	270,089
1730	8,256	1840	312,710
1756	10,530	1845	371,280
1774	22,861	1850	515,394
1786	23,688	1855	629,810
1790	33,131	1860	813,669
1800	60,489	1865	726,386
1805	75,587	1870	942,292
1810	96,373	1875	1,046,037

*The census returns of 1865 are universally acknowledged to have been inaccurate.

The Street System.

Like all of our older cities, New York at first spread its streets and avenues in any direction that seemed at the time most convenient. The original settlers had no conception of the ultimate destiny of their town, and they built their stores and houses wherever they pleased and with little regard to the street traffic. The result was that the lower and older part of the city, south of Houston street, became occupied in no particular order, and to-day is more or less irregular. The first streets were laid out at right angles with the water fronts, and as these were not parallel the streets did not meet at right angles. North of Houston street the city is laid out on an admirable plan that is at once simple, convenient and easily understood. Manhattan Island being long and narrow readily conformed to the American plan of streets at right angles. North and south the larger axis of the Island are the twelve great avenues that extend its entire length. In addition to these are a number of shorter avenues that extend part of the way each. These avenues are numbered and lettered from east to west. The most easterly, of the long avenues, is Avenue A. East of this, however, are three shorter avenues called B, C, and D, and named from west to east. The other avenues are numbered from the east. First Avenue is next west of Avenue A; Second is next west of this; Third, Fourth, Fifth, Sixth, Seventh, Eighth, Ninth, Tenth, and Eleventh follow in regular order till Twelfth is reached at the water side on the west. Besides these are two shorter avenues—Madison, between Fourth and Fifth, and Lexington, between Third and Fourth. These avenues are parallel and are wide streets.

Extending northward from the Battery to Central Park is Broadway, the great thoroughfare of the city. It passes through the center of the lower part of the city, in a straight line to Tenth street, and then crossing the avenues diagonally it continues in a northwest direction till it joins Eighth Avenue at 59th street. Beyond this point it follows the line of the old Bloomingdale road and assumes the name of the Boulevard. The streets crossing the Island and the avenues above Houston street are numbered from First street northward. One street in ten is made of double width, and twenty of the blocks between these streets average a mile. Fifth Avenue, in the center of the Island, divides each of these cross-streets into two parts known as East and West, as East 14th street, West 51st street, etc. In marking the streets numerals are used, numbering from Fifth Avenue each way east and west, as, East 19, West 45, etc. The avenues are marked Second Ave., Fourth Ave., Avenue D, etc., and these numerals and names may be found on the street lamps on the corners. Hence it is easy to understand the street system, and

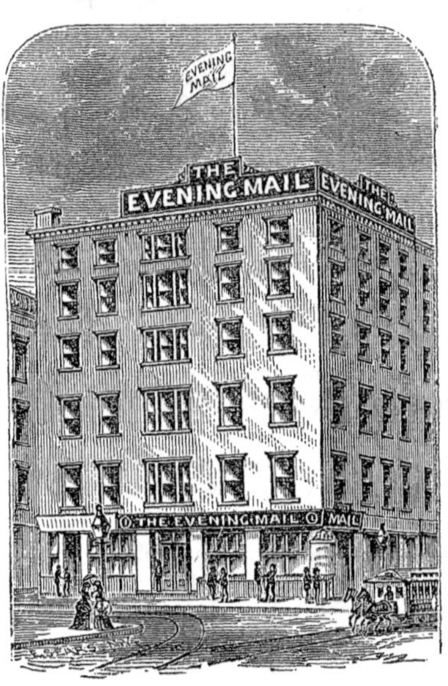

EAST BROADWAY AND BEEKMAN ST.

New York Stock Exchange,
No. 19 Broad Street.

the stranger is able to find any required locality quickly and readily. The numbering of the stores and houses is equally simple. On the avenues the numbers are continuous from south to north. On the cross-streets the numbers extend west on streets west of Fifth Avenue, and east on the other side. The numbers begin at Fifth Avenue at No. 1, and go to Sixth Avenue. Here a break is made, and the numbers begin at 100. At Seventh Avenue the numbers begin at 200. At Eighth Avenue the numbers begin at 300 and so on. Going east the numbers begin at 1 next Fifth Avenue; 100 at Fourth Avenue, and so on, the odd numbers being on the north side and the even numbers on the south of the cross streets. For instance, 326 West 57th street is on the south side of West 57th street, between Eighth and Ninth Avenues. No. 141 East 21st street is on the north side of the street, between Fourth and Third Avenues. Central Park, extending from 59th street to 110th street, and from Fifth Avenue to Eighth Avenue makes a blank in this street plan so that nearly all the streets between these, and Sixth and Seventh Avenues are cut in two. 65th, 79th, 85th and 97th streets, however, cross under the Park and ample roads continue the avenues north and south. These great avenues are almost wholly devoted to business, and above First street the cross-streets are occupied by dwelling-houses. This makes the streets quiet and agreeable, and at the same time places all the stores within easy reach. Below 14th street all the streets are invaded by business, and below Houston street warehouses and manufactories claim very nearly all of the space. To get a good idea of the character of New York City it is best to walk or ride through the great avenues. All the public buildings, churches, stores and institutions, are on the avenues or so near them as to be easily found, and to see them all, each avenue may be taken in turn, beginning with the most important.

BROADWAY.

This great thoroughfare begins at the crescent-shaped Park known as the

Battery.

This was the site of old Fort George, and is now merely a water-side Park and the emigrant landing station. The round building on the west side was a round fort known as Castle Clinton. It was given up to the city in 1823, and was afterwards converted into an opera house, where Jenny Lind first sang in this country, and finally became the landing place or reception room for the emigrants arriving at the Port. Here the new comers are properly cared for on arrival and are despatched on their various journeys over the country. The view from the

BROADWAY, SOUTH FROM BARCLAY ST. AND POST OFFICE.

Battery over the Bay is one of great beauty and animation, and the Park is well worth a brief visit. The buildings about it are of the older types. All are occupied as warehouses or hotels, and some were celebrated places in Revolutionary times. Broadway begins at the northeastern corner of the Battery, opposite the circle known as

Bowling Green.

Here once stood a leaden statue of George III., but it was happily made into good bullets for Continental muskets in 1776.

Kemp's Building,
Corner Cedar and William Sts.

The place is now neatly planted with trees and shrubbery. Opposite this, on the west, are old buildings once occupied by Generals Gage and Cornwallis and afterwards by Washington. Now they are devoted to steamship agencies and express offices. There is a slight rise in the roadway and at the top of the hill stands

Trinity Church.

This noble church standing opposite the head of Wall Street, was erected in 1846. It is 80x146 feet and 60 feet high. The tower is 284 feet high, and visitors are allowed to ascend it and enjoy the fine view from the spire. The building is open to the public every day and is well worth a visit. Trinity Church yard adjoins the church and is interesting on account of its monuments. Wall Street, famous for its banks and brokers' offices, here enters Broadway and the entire neighborhood is devoted to banking and insurance. Above the church the old stores give place to the immense structures of modern times. The *Equitable Life Insurance Building*, of Doric and Renaissance architecture, on the corner of Cedar street, the *American Bank Note Co.'s* building, on the corner of Liberty street, the gigantic palace, in composite style, of the *Western Union Telegraph Company*, on the corner of Dey street, the *Evening Post Building* on the corner of Fulton street, and many others here unite to present a sight unequaled in the world. Nowhere in the world can so many

EVENING POST BUILDING.

lofty and expensive buildings be found clustered in so small a space.

St. Paul's Chapel,

between Dey and Vesey streets, was built in 1766, and is 51x151 feet with a spire 203 feet high. Several monuments and inscriptions of historical interest are to be seen in the yard, beside the church. Opposite is the elegant white marble building of the

AMERICAN WATCH CO.'S BUILDING.
140, 142 and 146 Broadway, cor. of Liberty St.

Park Bank. Adjoining it is the *New York Herald* building on the corner of Ann Street. Next, north of St. Paul's, between Vesey and Barclay streets and fronting the junction of East Broadway (Park Row) and Broadway, is the famous *Astor House Hotel.*

The Post Office

stands in the triangular end of the old City Hall Park, between Broadway and East Broadway, and is not only a substantial and elegant structure of Doric and Renaissance architecture, but the largest public building in the city. Its dimensions are 144 feet

POST OFFICE.

front on the south, 279 feet on the Park, and 262½ feet on both the Broadway and East Broadway sides. The U. S. Government Supreme, Circuit and District Court-rooms are in the upper part of the building. East Broadway (formerly Park Row), the street that opens to the right, is mainly devoted to newspapers and makes the terminus of a number of horse railroads. The scene here in the middle of the day is past description. The enormous traffic, the crowds on the walks, the frantic haste that seems to possess every animated thing, the variety of men and teams and the general uproar and confusion, make a picture as peculiar as it is original. Here is a bit of New York intensified, a type of the whole country, and a thoroughly American scene. Passing the Post Office we come to

City Hall Park.

This was the first park laid out in the city. It formerly covered about 10 acres, bounded on the east by Park Row and

Centre street, by Chambers street on the north, and by Broadway on the west. It contains the City Hall, the new Court House, the Halls of Records, and other public offices.

The City Hall.

This building faces the south, and is a good sample of public building in the Italian style. It is 216x105 feet and 65 feet high, surmounted by a tower. The city government holds its meetings here, and here are the rooms of the chief public servants. In the Governor's Room are preserved a number of relics of the Revolution of some historical value and well worth a short visit. In the rear of the City Hall is

The New Court House.

This building was begun in 1861 and is still unfinished. It is occupied in part by various courts, and makes one of the most costly and sumptuous structures of the kind in the country. It is 250x150 feet, and is to be surmounted by a dome 170 feet high. Other public buildings devoted to the city service stand near. The neighborhood of the Park is rich in fine stores and offices. Just east of the Park is the site of the old Brick Church, built in 1767. It was used as a jail by the British during the Revolution, and finally was turned into a hospital. The site is now occupied by the *Times* and *World* building. Just here, on what is called Printing House Square, stands a fine bronze *Statue of Franklin.* The immense structure, with a lofty tower, is the *Tribune* Building. It is built of brick, stone and iron, in composite style, and

STAATS ZEITUNG, EAST BROADWAY AND CENTRE ST.

is surmounted with a tower 85 feet in height. The building is fire-proof, and is the highest in New York. At the north end of the Square, at the junction of East Broadway and Centre street, is the handsome granite building of the *Staats Zeitung*, with statues

New York Life Insurance Company's Building, 346 & 348 Broadway, New York.

of Franklin and Guttenburg above its portal. North of the Park, on the east corner of Chambers street and Broadway, is the great *A. T. Stewart wholesale store.* On the corner of Broadway and Warren street is one of the great stores of *Devlin & Co.*, the largest and one of the most reliable clothing houses in the city. All the stores and other buildings here are of the largest size and of most substantial construction, and the journey, continued up Broadway, opens a long and wonderful series of business palaces. The view up the street from this point gives one a good idea of the extent of the city and forms a good picture of its buisy life. Grace Church spire ends the long vista, while lines of omnibuses and the vast crowds of people give animation and life to the wonderful scene. At the corner of Leonard street may be seen the beautiful marble building of the *New York Life Insurance Co.*, in the Ionic style. From this point it descends to Canal street on a gentle incline and then rises again slightly. A detailed list of all the buildings would be only confusing and wearisome, and remarkable as this part of Broadway is for costly and spacious stores, none of them need special mention. The lower part of the street is almost exclusively devoted to the wholesale dry goods interest. Above Canal street the bustle and confusion, in a measure, subsides, and the dry goods people give way to the millinery and small warehouses. Retail stores appear and some of the great book stores are met. The famous clothiers, *Devlin & Co.*, occupy the fine store on the southwest corner of Grand street, and the great dry-goods house of *Cochran, McLean & Co.*, the building on the northeast corner. *St. Nicholas Hotel*, on the west side, between Broome and Spring streets, and the *Metropolitan Hotel*, on the east side, on the corner of Prince street, are the first of the great hotels of the city.

COR. BROADWAY AND WARREN ST.

The *Grand Central Hotel*, on the west side, between Bleecker and Amity streets, and *Brooks Brothers'* clothing store, on the corner of Bond street, are both notable buildings. *The American Watch Co.'s building* in Bond street, near Broadway, is worthy of attention. The retail trade here fills all the stores, and the character of the crowds on the walks changes rapidly. The book stores increase in number and the shop windows begin to make displays of marvelous attractiveness. *A. T. Stewart & Co.'s* immense iron store, occupying the entire square on the east side of Broadway between 9th and 10th streets, makes a most imposing show, and the long lines of carriages drawn up at its doors give

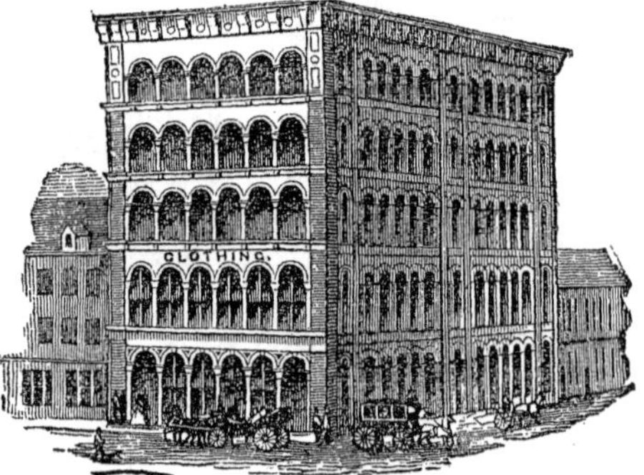

DEVLIN & CO., CLOTHIERS, COR. BROADWAY AND GRAND ST.

a brilliant and peculiar aspect to the street. Rival stores spread their varied charms on every side and throngs of shoppers fill the sidewalks. This is the beginning of the retail trade and the grand entrance to the court end of the town. Many of the most famous institutions, libraries, theaters and places of resort are in this neighborhood, and the dwellings of the people begin to fill the cross-streets. Grace Church, built in 1845, and a fine specimen of church architecture, stands on the corner of 10th street, and makes a fit ending to this part of Broadway. The views both up and down are fine, and serve to give the great avenue an artistic finish rarely possessed by city streets. From this corner Broadway turns slightly to the west of north. Both sides of the way are lined with stores devoted to pictures, music, dry goods, furniture, fancy goods, and aught else heart could wish or money

Methodist Book Concern's Building, Cor. Broadway and 11th Street, New York.

buy. Wallack's Theater, on the corner of East 13th street, is the first of the up-town and high-class theaters, and at the next block, on 14th street, Broadway enters

Union Square.

This Square extends from East 14th street to East 17th street. Fourth Avenue makes its eastern boundary and Broadway follows its western side. In the center is an oval planted with grass and

METROPOLITAN HOTEL.

trees and ornamented with a fountain. On 17th street is a broad plaza for reviewing troops, etc. On 14th street, to the east, is the *Equestrian Statue of Washington*, and on the west the *Bronze Statue of Lincoln*. Union Square was once the residence of the more fashionable people. It is now invaded by stores and hotels and is devoted to business. On entering the square from Broadway the *Union Square Theater* and the *Union Place Hotel* may be found on 14th street, a few doors to the east. A few steps beyond Fourth Avenue on 14th is the white marble façade of *Steinway & Son's* piano-forte warerooms; the *Academy of Music* on the corner of Irving Place, and still beyond *Tammany Hall*, both of them buildings celebrated in their way. On the west corner of Broadway and 14th street is the tall iron building of the *Domestic Sewing Machine Co.*, and next to which is the fine dry-goods store, *Le Boutillier Brothers*. One door west is the elegant structure of the *Wheeler and Wilson Manufacturiug Company*. On the west

ST. NICHOLAS HOTEL, Broadway, between Broome and Spring Streets.

side of the Square, just above 14th street is the *Spingler House*, and on the corner of 15th street is *Tiffany & Co.'s* great iron store, a vast museum of silverware, jewelry and articles of elegance. On Fourth Avenue, on the corner of 15th street, is the *Union Square Hotel.* On the north side of the square, on the corner of 17th street, is the *Everett House.* Beyond Union Square Broadway continues in a northwesterly direction, and is crowded with stores of every variety. The great dry-goods establishments of *Arnold, Constable & Co.*, on the corner of 19th street, and *Lord & Taylor*, on the corner of 20th, and *J. & C. Johnson*, on the cor-

LORD AND TAYLOR'S RETAIL STORE.
Cor. Broadway and 20th St.

ner of 22d streets, make this part of Broadway very attractive and equal to any street of its character in the world. At 21st and 22d streets are the *Madison Square* and *St. Germain Hotels*, and near the corner of 22d street is the *Park Theater*. At 23d street Broadway crosses Fifth Avenue and skirts the western side of

THE GRAND UNION HOTEL,

SARATOGA SPRINGS.

The Largest and most Magnificent in all its appointments of any in the World.

Madison Square.

This open space, liberally supplied with trees, lawns and walks, makes one of the most attractive and striking features of New York. On the east is the famous Madison Avenue, the home of wealth and refinement, Broadway touches its southwest corner, and the grand Fifth Avenue, known half round the world, forms its western side. East 23d and East 25th streets make its southern and northern limits. On every side may be seen hotels that are palaces, club-houses, costly beyond description, and churches and private dwellings that would be an honor to any city. Long vistas, open up and down three of the most remarkable streets in the country, while the life, animation and variety offered at every moment bewilder and charm the intelligent observer. At the southwest corner of the Square, at the junction of Broadway and Fifth Avenue and 23d street, stands the great marble pile of the *Fifth Avenue Hotel.* On the corner of 24th street, stands the well-known *Albemarle Hotel*, and at 25th street is the celebrated *Hoffman House.* At the triangle between Broadway, Fifth Avenue and 24th street, stands the stone shaft erected by the city to the memory of *General Worth.* Immediately behind it is the palatial building of the *New York Club.* From this point Broadway continues northwesterly towards Sixth Avenue. Concerning the other building on the eastern and northern sides of Madison Square, more may be found under the head of "Fifth Avenue" and "Madison Avenue," on another page. Continuing up Broadway we find a number of first-class stores, and pass the *St. James' Hotel*, on the corner of West 26th street. Between 27th and 28th streets, on the east side of Broadway, is the *Crittenden Hotel.* On the southeast corner of 27th street is the gigantic *Stevens Family Hotel*, one of the most lofty and palatial structures in the country. On the northwest corner is the *Coleman House.* A few steps west of Broadway, on 28th street, is the fashionable *Fifth Avenue Theater.* On the east side of Broadway, above 28th street, is the *Sturtevant House*, and on the corner of 29th street rises the towering front of the *Gilsey House.* On the corner of 31st street is the well-known *Grand Hotel*, and near the same corner is the *Winchester House.* Near 30th street is *Wood's Museum*, one of the minor theaters. At 34th street Broadway crosses Sixth Avenue, and at the base of the triangular park between the two streets at 32d St., is the beautiful marble building of the

FIFTH AVENUE HOTEL, Madison Square, Fifth Avenue and 23d Street, Worth Monument.

Dime SavingsBank. On the corner of West 33d street stands the imposing *Broadway Tabernacle*, Rev. Dr. Taylor, Pastor. Beyond this point Broadway is in a transition state. This is the limit of the fashionable retail trade, and the street is partly filled with an inferior class of stores, partially occupied with new family hotels and is partially unimproved. At 42d street are the *St. Cloud* and *Rossmore Hotels.* The *Albany, Saratoga*, and *Newport* are on the corners of W. 52d street, the *Rockingham* at West 56th, and the *Paris* at West 57th street, all family hotels. At West 59th street Broadway touches Eighth Avenue and ends at the circle and the *Boulevard.* Here is one of the entrances to Central Park, and the neighborhood seems in time destined to be one of the great fashionable centers of the city. The *Circle Hotel* occupies the block between Eighth Avenue and Broadway, and makes a fit ending to this remarkable street. Beyond this, the Boulevard, a wide avenue handsomely laid out, continues along the west side of the city, and over the heights of the Hudson, to Spuyten Duyvil Creek and into Westchester County.

Fifth Avenue.

Next to Broadway this is the most important and interesting street in New York. It is a broad, straight street, beginning at Washington Square in Waverley Place, and extending in a northerly direction, past the east side of Central Park, to Mount Morris Park, in Harlem. It is closely built up as far as 59th street, and beyond this point is being rapidly occupied. It already represents four miles of costly and elegant residences and churches, and is the one grand street to visit, even if nothing else is seen in the city. More beautiful than Broadway, it presents a charming succession of fine buildings, and an endless procession of people, and turnouts rivaling anything of the kind in the world, and if it lacks the animation and stir of the more popular and great business street, it amply compensates in finish and artistic effect. Beginning at *Washington Square* the first building of interest seen is the *Brevoort House*, on the N. E. corner of 8th street, one of the most elegant hotels in New York, C. C. Waite proprietor. It is celebrated for its quiet and refined surroundings, the superior excellence of the cuisine department, and the cultivated class of patrons it attracts.

At 9th street is *the Berkeley*, a new family hotel, and on the

ROSSMORE HOTEL, Broadway, 42d St. and Seventh Ave., New York, three blocks west of Grand Central Depot, CHARLES E. LELAND, Proprietor. Also Proprietor of the famous *Delavan Hotel* of Albany and the celebrated *Clarendon Hotel* of Saratoga Springs, N. Y. Prices, $4.00 per day.

N. W. corner of 10th street is the *Church of the Ascension*, Rev. John Cotton Smith, Rector. On the opposite corner is the "*Grosvenor*," a family hotel. On the west side of the avenue, between 11th and 12th streets, is the *First Presbyterian Church.* On the N. E. corner of 14th street is *Delmonico's Restaurant*, the most celebrated establishment in New York. At 12th street is the *Heath House*, arranged in flats. At the N. W. corner of 18th street, is the new *Chickering Music Hall*, and the warerooms for the pianoforte house of Chickering & Son. A few steps above, at 21st street, is the *Manhattan Club House.* At 22d street is the *Art Gallery* of *Knoedler Co.*, formerly Goupil's, and, just above, those of *Snedecor & Co.* and *Cottier & Co.* Another celebrated art establishment is passed at No. 144, on the west side. At 23d street Fifth Avenue crosses Broadway, and touches the west side of Madison Square. This square is mentioned elsewhere, under the chapter on Broadway. The celebrated *Fifth Avenue Hotel* occupies the corner of 23d street, and at the N. E. corner of 26th street, just beyond the Square, is the

BRUNSWICK HOTEL, FIFTH AV. AND TWENTY-SIXTH ST.

sumptuous *Brunswick House.* The *Stevens Family Hotel*, mentioned under the head of Broadway also, presents a fine front on Fifth Avenue, at the corner of West 27th street. There are very

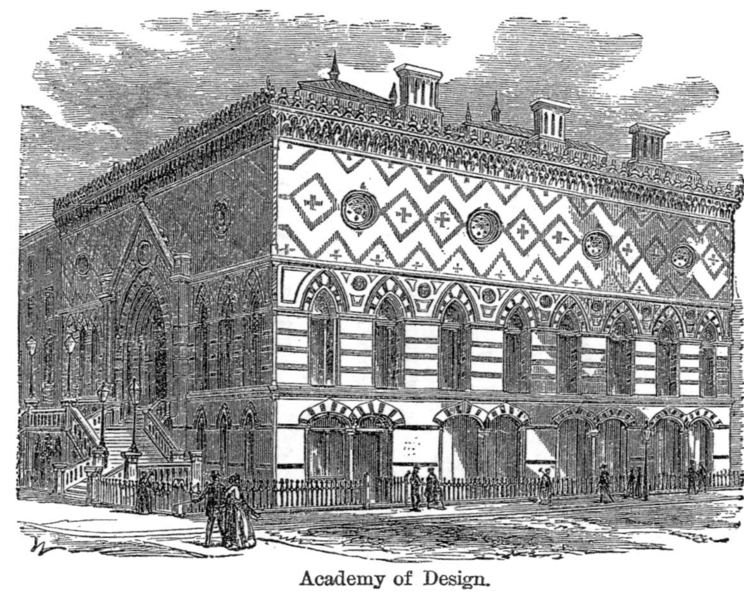

Academy of Design.

few stores on Fifth Avenue, and beyond this point they cease almost entirely, and the street is given up to the residences of the more wealthy people of the city. The street here is lined with trees, and each block seems to rival the others in richness of material and profusion, and splendor of architectural ornamentation. The church on the corner of West 29th street, is the *Collegiate Dutch Reformed*, Rev. Dr. Ormiston, Pastor. The small stone church on the corner of East 35th street is *Christ's Church*. At the corner of West 37th street is the *Brick Church*, belonging to the Presbyterian denomination. Fifth Avenue here climbs the gentle elevation known as Murray Hill, and affords a magnificent exhibition of New York wealth and luxury. The beautiful churches, costly residences, and palatial hotels, that for the next mile line the streets, present a sight rarely met with in the world. The most wealthy and noted families of the city live hereabouts. The two brick houses on the west side of the street, and between West 33d and 34th streets, are the residences of the *Astor family*. The great white marble palace on the northwest corner of West 34th street, is the residence of the late Mr. *Alexander T. Stewart*, and at the southeast corner of 41st street, is the home of *Wm. B. Vanderbilt*. The curious building on the east side between 41st and 42d Streets, is the *Rutgers Institute*, while opposite is the massive stone *Croton Reservoir*. At the corner of East 43d street, stands the beautiful *Jewish Temple*. This building, with its double towers and profuse and elaborate decoration, stands in high contrast to the Christian churches, and makes one of the most remarkable features of the avenue. At the corner of West 45th street, is the plain brown stone church, made famous through the eloquence of its pastor, *Rev. E. H. Chapin*. The single tower just above East 45th street, marks the entrance to the beautiful church known as the *Church of the Heavenly Rest*. Just beyond, and filling the front of block between 46th and 47th streets, stands the celebrated *Windsor Hotel*, one of the most elegant and costly hotels in the world. At the corner of West 48th street, is the highly ornate and striking *Dutch Reformed Church*, and at the corner of 50th street is the new *Buckingham Hotel*. Filling the entire space between 50th and 51st streets, is the immense *St. Patrick's Cathedral*, the largest and finest edifice of the kind in America. Though unfinished, it is a marvel of architectural beauty, and if the visitor sees nothing

WINDSOR HOTEL. FIFTH AVENUE and 46th STREET.

else in New York, this will amply repay the trouble of a visit. To understand its vast size and to see all its wonderful beauty, the visitor should walk round the Square and view every side. The best view of the east end is obtained from the southeast corner of 50th street and Madison Avenue. The next church on Fifth Avenue is *St. Thomas' Church*, at the corner of 53d Street. At the Square, between 54th and 55th streets, stand the buildings of *St. Luke's Hospital*, and on the corner of 55th street is the new *Fifth Avenue Presbyterian Church*, better known as *Dr. Hall's.* From this point to 59th street, Fifth Avenue is lined with a number of remarkably fine private residences, and there the grand avenue touches Central Park, at the Scholars' Gate. Beyond this, the avenue keeps on the east side of the Park, and ultimately reaches Harlem. The avenue is not wholly built up and presents few objects of interest, except the *Lenox Library*, between 70th and 71st Streets.

Madison and Lexington Avenues.

Though these avenues are not classed among the great avenues, as they are somewhat shorter, they rank next to Fifth Avenue in interest and importance. Madison Avenue begins at East 23d street, at the southern end of Madison Square, and extends north between Fourth and Fifth Avenues to Harlem. Lexington Avenue, including Irving Place, begins at East 14th street and extends north between Fourth and Fifth Avenues to 63d street. They are, as it were, extra avenues inserted for a short distance between the great avenues, and both are more or less occupied by the residences of the more wealthy people. Madison Avenue has a number of fine churches that may be briefly pointed out in order, beginning at Madison Square. The first is the *Madison Square Presbyterian Church*, on the southeast corner of 24th street. At the southeast corner of 26th street is the handsome building of the *Union League Club*. The ugly building filling the entire block between 26th and 27th streets was erected by Mr. P. T. Barnum, as a place for his popular exhibitions and for Summer concerts, and is now known as the "*Hippodrome*." The meetings of the celebrated revivalists, Moody and Sankey, were held here in the Winter of 1876. At the northwest corner of 28th street is the *Church of the Atonement*, and at the southwest corner of 29th is the *Rutgers Presbyterian.* The small church at the other corner of the same street

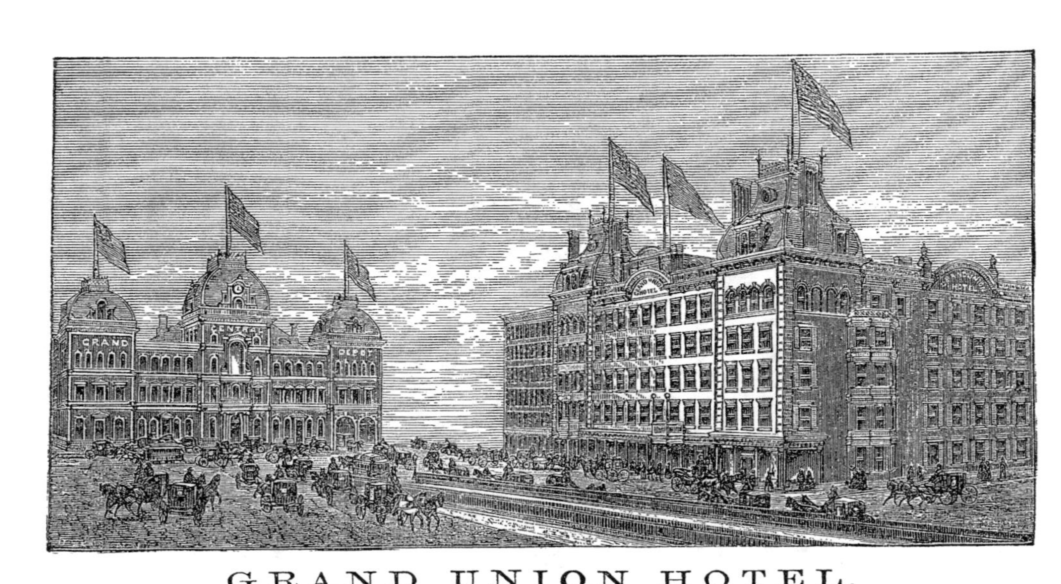
GRAND
CENTRAL
DEPOT
HOTEL

is the *Church of the Transfiguration*, popularly known as "*The Little Church round the Corner*." At 35th street is *Zion's Church*, and at the corner of 42d street is the beautiful *Church of the Hol. Trinity.* At 44th street stands *St. Barthblomew's*, one of the most elegant churches in the city, and at the corner of 45th street the *Church of the Disciples.* This church is built of iron, and is more curious than beautiful, though it is one of the most popular in New York. At the corner of 53d street is the 53d street *Memorial Presbyterian Church.* At 70th street may be seen the beautiful *Lenox Hospital*, erected through the liberality of James Lenox; and at 89th street is the *St. Luke's Home* and the *Church of the Beloved Disciple*, among the most interesting buildings in the city. Aside from these, Madison Avenue presents nothing special beyond this point.

Lexington Avenue.

This avenue naturally includes Irving Place, that begins at East 14th street and extends north between Third and Fourth Avenues to East 20th street at Gramercy Park. At the other side of this small park the street is continued under the name of Lexington Avenue, as far north as *Hamilton Square*, at East 66th street. It is closely built up with dwellings of the better class, as far as 59th street and though neither Irving Place nor the avenue contain many public buildings, they are both interesting as places of residences. At 14th street is the *Academy of Music*, a large building of rather forbidding aspect, and the largest theater in the city. At the corner of 15th street is *Irving Hall*, used for concerts and public meetings. At the northwest corner of East 16th street is the *Westminster Hotel.* At 20th street Irving Place ends at *Gramercy Park.* Beyond the park the first building of importance on Lexington Avenue is the *College of the City of New York*, occupying a large brick building in the Gothic style on the southeast corner of 23d street. Beyond this point the avenue is entirely occupied by dwellings, and makes a fine quiet street for the better class of residences. The church on the corner of 35th street is the *Church of St. John the Baptist.*. At the corner of 42d street is the *Asylum for Cripples.* Just west of Lexington avenue, in East 44th street, are the spacious and well-arranged *Storage Warehouses of Messrs. Cornelius O'Reilly & Brothers.* They are the largest and best in New York. Above this street the avenue is being rapidly built up. It contains a few churches and at 66th street may be seen the fine buildings of the *Mount Sinai Hospital.* Beyond this there is nothing of special interest.

Fourth Avenue and Bowery.

Fourth Avenue is a continuation of the old thoroughfare known as the Bowery, and the two streets combined make the longest continuous street in the city, extending from Chatham street in the

LEXINGTON STORAGE WAREHOUSE.

lower part of the city northward to Harlem River, a distance of 9 miles. Above 42d street Fourth Avenue is occupied by the immense Fourth Avenue Tunnel, an open cut occupied by the railroads centering at the *Grand Central Depot.* At 34th street there is a tunnel for the horse railroads, extending to 42d street, and the street above is known for that distance as Park Avenue. The Bowery extending from Chatham street to 6th street is wholly devoted to business. It is a wide street and somewhat noted for the immense traffic crowding it all times. The stores are generally of the second and third class, and it contains no buildings of importance or special value, except the *Dry Dock Savings Bank* at the corner of Third street. The Bowery is worth inspecting as a curious sample of certain phases of New York life and business and as illustration of the enterprise and industry of the great middle class of people. Fourth Avenue begins at the junction of Third Avenue and the Bowery. The great stone building standing between the two avenues is the *Cooper Union*. At the block between 8th and 9th streets is the great brick building known as the *Bible House*. On the west side between 9th and 10th street is Stewart's great up-town retail store. At the corner of 14th treet is the *German Savings Bank*. Here Fourth Avenue passes along the eastern side of Union Square. The warerooms of *Steinway and Sons* may here be seen on 14th street, while the *Union Square Hotel* comes just above at 15th street. At 17th street facing Union Square is the *Everett House*, and on the corner of 18th is the *Clarendon*, one of the oldest and best hotels in New York. At 20th street is the Unitarian Church presided over by Rev. Dr. Bellows, and known as *All Souls' Church*. At 21st street is *Calvary Church*, belonging to the Episcopalians, Rev. Dr. Washburn,

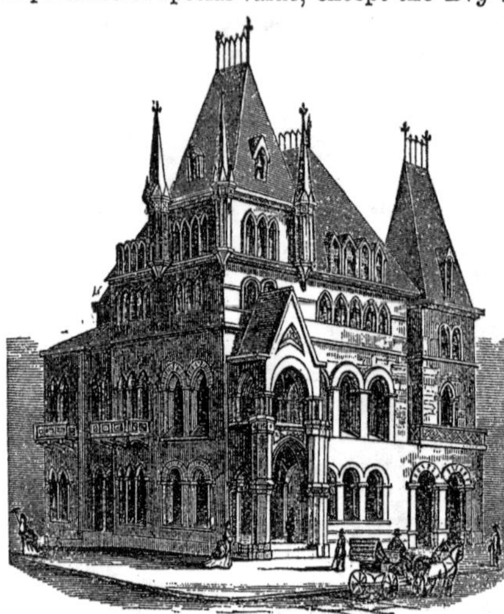

DRY DOCK SAVINGS BANK.
Cor. 3d St. and Bowery.

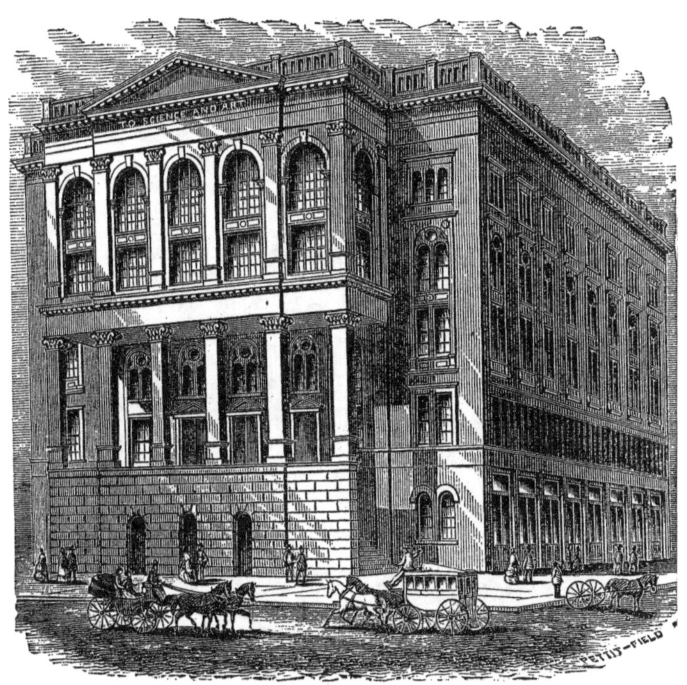

Cooper Union, for the Advancement of Science and Art,
Third and Fourth Avenues and Seventh and Eighth Streets.

Rector. On the northeast corner of 22d street, is *St. Paul's Methodist Episcopal Church*, and opposite, on the N. W. corner, is the *Fourth Avenue Presbyterian Church*, Rev. Dr. Crosby, Pastor

GERMAN SAVINGS BANK BUILDING.
Cor. of 4th Av. and 14th Street.

At the southwest corner of 23d street is the building of the *Young Men's Christian Association.* At the northwest corner is the *Academy of Design*, and on the northeast corner is the *New York College of Physicians and Surgeons.* A number of smaller hotels are passed, and at 26th street may be noticed the extended building known as the *Hippodrome*, and at 34th street the brick tunnel is reached, and the street that passes overhead is known as

Park Avenue.

This is merely a continuation of Fourth Avenue on the top of the hill. The horse railroad passes through the tunnel and Fourth Avenue is continued beyond. At 34th street may be seen the gigantic iron hotel, built by A. T. Stewart for a *Working Women's Home*. Park Avenue is occupied by a better class of houses than Fourth Avenue, and contains three handsome churches; the *Church of the Messiah* (Unitarian), at 34th street, the *Church of the Covenant* at 35th street, and the *First Baptist Church* at 39th street. At 41st street may be seen the popular *Grand Union Hotel* and the avenue reaches an apparent end at the immense

GRAND UNION HOTEL.

Grand Central Depot.

This is one of the largest and most imposing buildings in the country. It consists of a "head house" on 42d street, in which are the waiting rooms and general offices of the N. Y. and N. H. R. R. Co., a long continuation along the west side, containing the waiting rooms and general offices of the Harlem and N. Y. Central and Hudson River R. R's, and an immense iron "train house" seven hundred feet long, three hundred feet wide, and nearly one hundred feet high, covering all in one great span roof. The style is French, with Mansard towers, and, seen from the west or south, the building is both grand and striking. The interior, particularly at night, is impressive for its enormous size, its lightness of construction, and grace of outline, and the visitor should take pains to examine the building in all its details. A short distance to the right on 42d street is the *Asylum for Cripples*, occupying a curious looking building of brick and iron on the north side of the street. Beyond 42d street the yards of the three railroads that use the Grand Central Depot occupy Fourth Avenue as far as 50th street. Crossing from Madison Avenue to Lexington Avenue are a number of iron foot and carriage bridges. Beyond 50th street the railroad is sunk below the level of Fourth Avenue in an immense open cut and tunnel that makes one of the most remarkable pieces of railroad engineering to be found in the country. Visitors who have

METROPOLITAN SAVINGS BANK, 3D. AV. 7TH STREET.

time should not fail to examine this immense and most interesting work. At 50th street may be seen a portion of the buildings belonging to the *Columbia College and School of Mines* on the west side of the avenue. Opposite are the buildings of the *Women's Hospital* of the State of New York. At 52d street on the east

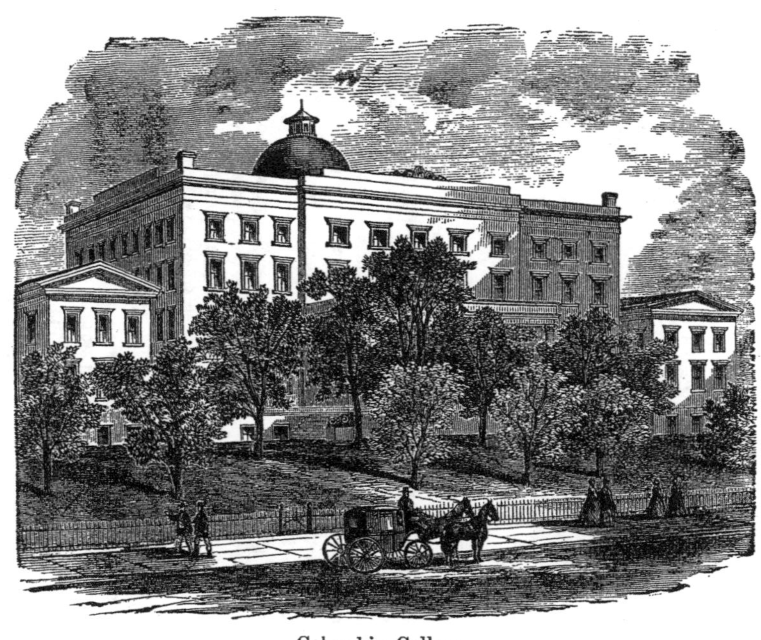

Columbia College,

Fiftieth Street, between Fourth and Fifth Avenues.

side of the avenue is *Steinway and Sons'* great piano-forte manufactory. At the corner of 69th street may be seen the *Normal College* a fine, red brick building in the Gothic style. This part of Fourth Avenue is only partially built up and presents nothing more of interest in this direction.

Third Avenue.

Third Avenue is one of the largest and most populous single streets in New York. It extends from the junction of Fourth Avenue and the Bowery at Sixth street, northward, between Fourth and Second Avenues, to Harlem River. More than six miles long in a perfectly straight line, solidly built up for almost the whole length, and wholly devoted to business, it makes one of the most remarkable streets in the world. Its wide road-way and ample sidewalks, its enormous traffic and the vast variety and extent of its commerce makes it well worth seeing, if for nothing more than its overflowing life and intense activity. At the same time it is not attractive in every respect, and may be called at once a sample of New York enterprise and municipal neglect. It shows no buildings of particular interest or importance, and is only of value to the visitor as an extensive New York thoroughfare and shop street.

Sixth Avenue

makes a second Broadway. It extends from Carmine street north, between Fifth and Sixth Avenues, to 59th street, at Central Park. Beyond the Park it goes on to the Harlem River. Below the Park it is solidly built up its entire length, and is wholly devoted to retail stores of the first class. Above the stores all the buildings are devoted to tenements and flats. Some of these are very elegant and expensive, and the whole aspect of the street suggests successful business enterprise and comfortable prosperity. Beyond the Park the avenue is only partly built up. The Sixth Avenue horse railroad occupies the avenue below 59th street, and everywhere the street is crowded with a large traffic. Though it does not present many public buildings of interest, it is one of the most famous thoroughfares in New York, and is well worth a visit on account of its life, animation, and business activity. Its miles of stores offer every attraction to the shopper, with the added charm of being a trifle more sensible in the mat-

BIBLE HOUSE (Astor Place), New York.

ter of prices than Broadway. The chief buildings of interest may be found in the lower part of the avenue. At West 14th street, a little to the left is the *Lyceum Theater*, and the *Metropolitan Museum of Art*, on opposite sides of 14th street. At the southeast corner of West 23d street is *Booth's Theater*, one of the most fashionable places of amusement in the city. On

MASONIC TEMPLE.
Sixth Av. and West 23d Street.

the opposite corner is the *Masonic Temple*, perhaps the most costly and magnificent building of its character in the country. Besides the Masonic Halls and offices, it contains the spacious and magnificent fire-proof rooms and vaults of the *Central Safe Deposit Co.* A few steps to the left, down West 23d street, is the new *Twenty-third Street Theater*. At 33d street is the new *Eagle Theater*, one of the most popular of its class. At 34th street Sixth Avenue crosses Broadway. At 40th street is the *Marlborough House*, and extending from 40th to 42d street is *Reservoir Park*. A number of small hotels may be found on this avenue, all of them more or less favorites with the traveling public.

Beyond this there is nothing of particular interest on this avenue, except its numerous and attractive stores.

Seventh Avenue.

This avenue begins at Greenwich Avenue near West 11th street, and extends north between Sixth and Eighth Avenues to 59th street, at Central Park. It is more quiet than Sixth or Eighth Avenues, and is partly occupied by stores and dwelling-houses. The business portion extends to about 42d street, and from there to 50th it is lined with dwellings. Above that it is not wholly built up. At 58th street is the famous *Central Park Garden*, the summer-home of the Thomas orchestra, and the most noted public resort of its kind in the country. There are few public buildings of any account on this avenue, and it is chiefly interesting as making the best entrance to Central Park for visitors on foot. The Broadway line of horse-cars use the upper part of this avenue jointly with the Seventh Avenue line, and take passengers to the same gate of the Park and to the Thomas' Garden.

Eighth Avenue.

This long and busy avenue begins at Greenwich Street, at Abingdon Square, and extends northerly past Central Park along its western side to Central Bridge over the Harlem River at a point once known as "McComb's Dam." The only building of special interest in the lower part of the avenue is the *Grand Opera House* at the corner of West 23d street. Beyond this point the avenue is entirely devoted to retail trade. A walk through the place of a Saturday evening gives one of New York's most peculiar sights. The petty trade that crowds every store and clings to the edge of every walk, is something wonderful, while the vast throngs of people out shopping by gas-light are more wonderful still. Above 50th street a better class of stores and more expensive residences appear. At 59th street, 8th Avenue, Broadway, and the Boulevard unite in a circle or circus. A fine hotel fills one side and one of the entrances to Central Park, fancifully called the "Merchant's Gate," makes another. To the left a short distance down 59th street may be seen the picturesque towers and buildings of the *Roosevelt Hospital*. Beyond 59th street, 8th Avenue follows the western edge of Central Park its entire length and passing the gates at 72d, 79th, 85th, 96th, 100th and 110th streets. This part of the avenue is not yet built up, and is lined with market gardens and the temporary shanties of the laboring population that "squats" in the unfinished squares. Beyond Central Park the avenue descends a long hill to the flats bordering Harlem River. Here views of High Bridge and the surrounding country may be obtained. At the river the avenue passes a few scattered blocks of houses and follows the old country road to Central Bridge leading to the main land. Beyond the river the Hudson River Railroad is crossed and the road enters the open country.

Other Avenues.

Besides the great avenues already mentioned there are a number of others of equal length, but of less interest to the stranger. At the east side of the city are the four shorter Avenues, known as Avenues A, B, C, and D. They each begin at Houston Street and extend northward to the East River. Avenue A is next east of First Avenue, Avenue B comes next, and C and D follow in order, each being shorter than the last. They are all occupied by a poorer class of houses and present no special features of interest. First Avenue and Second Avenue lie east of Third Avenue, and both begin at Houston street and extend northward to Harlem River between Third Avenue and the East River or Avenue A. They are compactly built up in the lower part, but opposite Central Park they are still more or less unfinished. The business and population has, for the most part, no particular interest for the visitor. On the west side of the city next west of Eighth Avenue, are Ninth, Tenth and Eleventh Avenues. Ninth Avenue is closely built up as far as 59th street, and is chiefly remarkable as the site of the New York Elevated Railroad. All of these avenues are occupied by shops and manufactories and by tenements for the immense population that throngs them at all times. The peculiar shape of New York city makes further description of the streets unnecessary. Broadway and the great avenues make its business thoroughfares, its residences are mainly on the cross streets that intersect the island from east to west.

PLACES OF AMUSEMENT.

It has been said, "London for business, Paris for pleasure, New York for both." However true this may be, it is certain

CONGRESS HALL, Saratoga Springs, N. Y. Hathorn & Cooke, Proprietors.

Opens June 1st.

Hathorn Spring, 75 feet north; Columbian Spring, 200 feet south; Congress Spring, 50 feet south; Hamilton Spring, 75 feet east.

that New York is abundantly supplied with amusements of every kind and quality. Its first-class theaters are equal to any in the world, and all the best talent that live in Europe eventually appears before our people. New York is a great center to which all artists, both musical and dramatic, look for their highest honors, and in turn they all appear here. There is no longer the slightest need to go abroad to hear and see "the great stars," for they are only too glad to shine here, at least once in their lives. Instead of America going to Europe, the cream of Europe comes to New York, and the visitor to this city has advantages of a cosmopolitan character in the way of entertainment the like of which cannot be found in London or Paris. Chief among New York places of amusement come the first-class theaters. Each may be briefly mentioned in order and the visitor can then select to suit himself. The prices vary greatly, but even at the best houses the charges are reasonably low. The **Fifth Avenue Theater,** located on 28th street near Broadway, is a select and fashionable resort, devoted to first-class dramatic performances, ably, correctly and tastefully given by the best artists. The dramas are generally of the modern society type, and are always perfectly unexceptionable in every respect.

Wallack's Theater, on Broadway near Union Square, is a handsome theater, devoted exclusively to first-class plays. The mounting and acting are invariably of the finest and most artistic. The plays generally belong to the highest modern school. The **Union Square Theater,** on Union Square, rivals the Fifth Avenue and Wallack's in point of artistic rendering of its performances. The company is maintained at a high standard and the plays given are always admirably presented. The dramas commonly belong to the modern French school.

Booth's Theater, on W. 23d St., near Sixth Ave., is one of the most elegant theaters in the world. It is celebrated for the perfection and accuracy with which its plays are presented. None but artists of the first class appear here, and, though there is much latitude in the selections of the plays, all are produced in a manner to satisfy the most exacting. The largest theater is the **Academy of Music,** 14th St. and Irving Place, devoted to opera and dramatic performances of the highest order. The **Park Theater,** is a popular resort among all classes. It is located on Broadway, near 22d street. Its plays are admirably presented and are generally American in character, both in action, scene and story. The

Lyceum Theater, on West 14th street near Sixth Avenues. Its plays and operas are commonly French, and are usually given in that language. All its performances are admirably acted and mounted. These seven theaters are all first-class in point of expense, and the sittings are about alike in price. Visitors will always find them open in the winter season, and may always rely on the very best dramatic and operatic entertainments that can be found in the country. Besides these theaters are a number of smaller houses, each attractions of more or less value. The

Stadt Theater, at 45 Bowery, is devoted to German plays.

Germania Theater, is another house devoted to the drama in the German language, and is located on East 14th street near Third Avenue. One of the largest theaters in New York is the

Grand Opera House, on Eighth Avenue and West 23d St.; it is open occasionally for spectacular and melodramatic performances.

Olympic Theater, No. 624 Broadway, is devoted to variety entertainment. The

Eagle Theater, on Sixth Avenue and Broadway, is a new and very pretty theater devoted to the lighter kinds of dramas.

Tony Pastor's new Theater, No. 585 Broadway, presents a variety of plays and sketches generally of a light order.

Wood's Museum, on Broadway near 30th street, usually offers popular melodramas, besides the attraction of the Museum itself.

Twenty-Third Street Theater, on West 23d street near Sixth Avenue, is devoted to sensational plays. Besides, these theaters are one or two others of less importance, but the above list is ample for the intelligent visitor, and will furnish amusement in variety for a number of nights. In Negro Minstrels there is one excellent entertainment of the usual stamp at the

San Francisco Minstrels, on Broadway near 28th street.

Steinway Hall, on East 14th St. near Broadway and Fourth Av., *Chickering Hall*, corner of Fifth Avenue and 18th street, and the *Academy of Music*, are the usual places devoted to concerts in the winter. First-class concerts are given at these places almost every night from October to June, and the particulars may be found in the daily papers.

The Central Park Garden, on Seventh Avenue near 59th St., is in the summer a resort for lovers of instrumental music.

The Hippodrome a vast building occupying the entire square between Madison and Fourth Avenues, E. 26th and E. 27th streets, is also devoted to music in the summer. Below is a tabulated alphabetical list of the principal places of amusement.

ACADEMY OF MUSIC	E. 14th St. and Irving Place.
ASSOCIATION HALL	E. 23d St. and Fourth Avenue.
BOOTH'S THEATER	W. 23d St. and Sixth Avenue.
BOWERY THEATER	Bowery, near Canal St.
CENTENNIAL THEATER	514 Broadway.
CENTRAL PARK GARDEN	W. 59th St. and Seventh Avenue.
CHICKERING HALL	W. 18th St. and Fifth Avenue.
EAGLE THEATER	Broadway and W. 32d Street.
FIFTH AVENUE THEATER	W. 28th St. near Broadway.
GERMANIA THEATER	E. 14th Street near Third Avenue....Tammany Hall.
GLOBE THEATER	Broadway, opp. Waverly Place.
GRAND OPERA HOUSE	W. 23d Street and Eighth Avenue.
HIPPODROME	E. 26th St. and Madison Avenue.
LYCEUM THEATER	West 14th St. west of Sixth Avenue.
METROPOLITAN THEATER	585 Broadway
NIBLO'S THEATER	Broadway, bet. Prince and Houston Sts.
OLYMPIC THEATER	Broadway, bet. Houston and Bleecker Sts.
PARK THEATER	Broadway, bet. 21st and 22d Sts.
PARISIAN VARIETIES, ROBINSON HALL	W. 16th St. bet. Broadway and Fifth Avenues.
SAN FRANCISCO MINSTRELS	Broadway, cor. 29th St.
STADT THEATER	Bowery, bet. Canal and Bayard Sts.
STEINWAY HALL	E. 14th St. near Fourth Avenue.
THIRD AVENUE THEATER	Third Avenue, bet. 32d and 33d Sts.
THIRTY-FOURTH STREET THEATER	E. 34th St., bet. 2d and 3d Avenues.
TIVOLI THEATER	East 8th St. bet. 2d and 3d Avenues.
TONY PASTOR'S THEATER	585 Broadway
TWENTY-THIRD STREET THEATER	W. 23d St. near Sixth Avenue.
UNION SQUARE THEATER	E. 14th St. near Broadway.
WALLACK'S THEATER	Broadway and 13th St.
WOOD'S MUSEUM	Broadway near 30th St.

ART GALLERIES.

New York, though not well supplied with free art galleries, has a number of art stores, all of which are open to the public, and these make up in part for the absence of a great gallery. The *Academy of Design* on the corner of E. 23d street and Fourth Avenue, is the largest and best gallery in the city. Exhibitions of paintings are held here at certain times in the year, and a small fee is charged at the door. The *Metropolitan Museum of Art*, devoted to painting, sculpture and ceramic art is open nearly all the year round, and is free to the public on Mondays. A fee is charged other days. The museum is fine, for one so recently founded, and is located on W. 14th street near Sixth Avenue. *Cooper Institute*, Free, Fourth Avenue and 8th St., and the *Historical Society*, Cor. Second Avenue and 11th St., where strangers are received by introduction, are interesting museums. In addition to these are a number of picture galleries

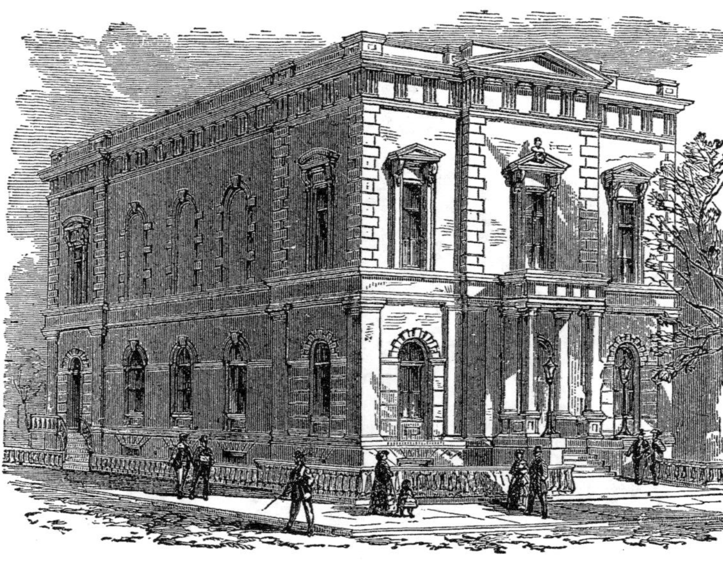

New York Historical Society,

Second Avenue, corner of Eleventh Street.

attached to picture stores, all of which are freely open to the public. *Knoedler & Co.'s, late Goupil's*, at the corner of 22d street and Fifth Avenue, is the most noted of these. *Cottier & Co.*, No. 144 Fifth Avenue, includes ceramic art, stained glass, and the higher kinds of household decorations. *Snedecor's* at Fifth Avenue, and *Schaus's* No. 749 Broadway, are devoted to oil paintings and engravings. At *H. Woods, Jr.'s.*, No. 826 Broadway, may be seen a large gallery of engravings and chromos. At *Kurtz's Photographic Gallery*, on 23d Street (Madison Square), is a fine gallery in which paintings of all kinds are often on exhibition. Besides these are a great number of lesser places, all of which display pictures of varying merit. At various times during the season, galleries of paintings are displayed at the various art auctions, due notice of which may be found in the daily papers.

LIBRARIES.

The *Astor Library*, founded by John Jacob Astor, in 1848, is free to all for reference, but none of the books can be taken from the building. It is located in Lafayette Place and numbers 148,000 volumes. The *Mercantile Library*, in Astor Place, is general in its character. It has a large reading-room and keeps its shelves well supplied with all the new books. It was established in 1848, and is free to its members only. It counts 148,000 volumes. The *Society Library*, in University Place, was organized in 1754. It has a library of 64,000 volumes, reading-room, etc. It is exclusively used by share-holders, and such others as may pay a small annual fee. The *Apprentice's Library*, belonging to the "General Society of Mechanics and Tradesmen of the City of New York," is free to apprentices; others pay a small fee. It is of a general character, numbering 50,000 volumes. The Library of the *Historical Society*, numbering 40,000, and the *Eclectic Library*, 30,000 volumes, stand next in importance. The *New York Institute Law Library*, in Chambers street, is open to members of the bar on payment of a small fee. It numbers 17,500 volumes exclusively on legal subjects. The *Cooper Union Library*, of a general character and numbering 12,600 volumes, is entirely free. It also includes a free reading room, both located in the Cooper Union at the junction of Fourth and Third Avenues. The *Library of the Association of the Bar* of New York, located in 27th street, was started in

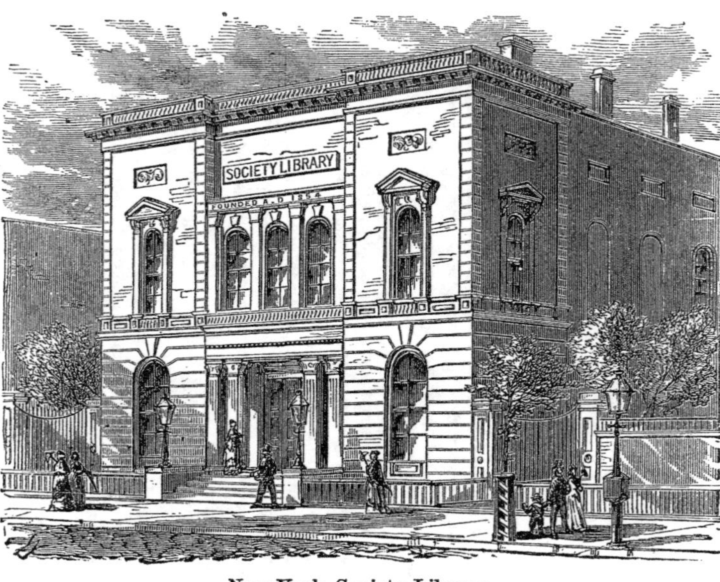

New York Society Library,
67 *University Place.*

1871 and now numbers 8,000 volumes. The *Geographical Society*, and the *American Institute*, have libraries of about 11,000 volumes each. The *Young Men's Christian Association* has a general library of 10,000 volumes in its building, on East 23d street, for the use of its members only. The *City Library*, in the City Hall, consists entirely of public documents, and is free to such as wish to consult its 4,000 books. The *Mott Memorial Library*, devoted to medical and scientific books, was founded by the widow of Dr. Valentine Mott. It numbers 4,000 volumes and is free. Besides these are the *Woman's Library*, in Bleecker street, numbering 3,000 volumes and free to working-women; the *Library of the Natural History Society*—5,000 vols.; the library of the *Medical Library and Journal Association*, in East 28th street—3,500 vols.; the Harlem Library—7,000 vols.; the *Printers' Library*—3,500 vols.; and the *Washington Heights Library*, with 2,500 volumes. The *Lenox Library*, occupying a magnificent building on Fifth Avenue between 70th and 71st streets, is not yet open to the general public, but promises to be one of the finest libraries in the city. We append a list:

APPRENTICES—472 Broadway.—Open from 8 A.M. to 9 P.M.

ASTOR.—Lafayette place, near Astor place. 9 A.M. to 5 P.M. Free.

CITY.—12 City Hall. Open daily, from 10 A.M. to 4 P.M. Free.

COOPER UNION.—Seventh, corner Fourth avenue. Free reading-rooms for males and females. Open from 9 A.M. to 9 P.M.

HARLEM.—Third avenue, near 122d. Open from 2 to 7 P.M.

LIBRARY OF THE AMERICAN INSTITUTE.—Cooper Union. Open daily, from 9 A.M. to 9 P.M., and on Wed. and Sat. from 9 A.M. to 7 P.M.

MERCANTILE LIBRARY ASSOCIATION.—Astor place. Open from 8 A.M. to 9 P.M. Down-town office, 51 Liberty. Terms of membership: For clerks, $1 initiation fee, and $4 per annum. Merchants and others, $5 annually. Reading-room open from 8 A.M. to 10 P.M.

MOTT MEMORIAL AND MEDICAL.—58 Madison av. 9 A.M. to 9 P.M.

NEW YORK HISTORICAL SOCIETY.—Second av., c. of E. 11th. Open October to April, 9 A.M. to 9 P.M.; April to October, 9 A.M. to 6 P.M.

NEW YORK LAW INSTITUTE.—41 Chambers. Open from 8.30 A.M. to 6 P.M. from March to October; rest of the year, from 9 A.M. to 5 P.M.

NEW YORK SOCIETY.—67 University place. Open from 8 A.M. until 6 P.M. Reading-room from 8 A.M. to 10 P.M.

PRINTERS.—3 Chambers. Open every Saturday P.M. Free.

WASHINGTON HEIGHTS.—Tenth av., n. W. 160th.

WOMEN'S.—38 Bleecker. Open daily, from 9 A.M. to 4 P.M.

YOUNG MEN'S CHRISTIAN ASSOCIATION.—Twenty-third st., c. Fourth av.; Third av. c. E. 122d; 245 Hudson; 473 Grand; and 285 Bleecker. Open daily from 8 A.M. to 10 P.M. Sundays from 1 to 9.30 P.M.

CITY OF NEW YORK.

CENTRAL PARK DIRECTORY.

CARRIAGES will leave the Merchants' Gate, 59th street and Eighth avenue, making the circuit of the Park, at brief intervals, from 7 a. m., till 9 p. m., and may be taken anywhere on the road.

Fare for each passenger making the entire circuit of the Park, or any distance, *Twenty-five cents.* The circuit will be made in about one hour and a half.

Not more than twelve persons will be allowed in a carriage at any one time. When the word "Full" is shown on the carriage, no passengers will be taken in.

Park-keepers in uniform are on duty at all hours of the day and night, and will give visitors information respecting the carriages and the Park.

No parcel or baggage is permitted in the carriages.

Smoking is not allowed in the carriages.

Parties will please report any incivility on the part of the driver, to a park-keeper, or to the Comptroller of the Park.

The Park is open every day in the year; the hours of opening and closing vary with the season.

Length of Park from 59th street to 110th street, about 2½ miles; width of the Park from Fifth avenue to Eighth avenue, about ½ mile; length of Park Carriage Roads, about 9½ miles; length of Park Bridle Roads, about 5½ miles; length of Park Walks, about 27½ miles.

The Park contains 862 acres; New Reservoir, 107 acres; Old Reservoir, 35 acres, Pond, 59th street and Sixth avenue, 5 acres, Lake, 20 acres; Conservatory Water, 2½ acres; Pool, 2 acres; Harlem Lake, 12 acres: Loch, 1.

The Gallery of Statuary and Art is at the old Chapel of Mount St. Vincent. near the north end of the Park.

The Zoölogical and Natural History Collections are at the Museum, near the south-east part of the Park.

Boats to take visitors around the Lake may be found at the various landings.

Refreshments may be obtained at the Casino and at Mount St. Vincent, and *Mineral Waters* at the "Springs."

Music on the Mall every Saturday afternoon, when the weather is fine.

While a drive around the Park is very interesting, yet many of its most attractive features can be seen only by taking the foot-paths.

LOCATION AND NAMES OF GATES.

5th av.	&	59th	st.	Scholars' Gate	8th av.	&	110th	st.	Strangers' Gate
6th "	"	59th	"	Artists' Gate	5th "	"	72d	"	Children's Gate
7th "	"	59th	"	Artisans' Gate	5th "	"	79th	"	Miners' Gate
8th "	"	59th	"	Merchants' Gate	5th "	"	90th	"	Engineers' Gate
8th "	"	72d	"	Woman's Gate	5th "	"	96th	"	Woodman's Gate
8th "	"	79th	"	Hunter's Gate	5th "	"	102d	"	Girls' Gate
8th "	"	85th	"	Mariner's Gate	5th "	"	110th	"	Pioneers' Gate
8th "	"	96th	"	Gate of All Saints	6th "	"	110th	"	Farmers' Gate
8th "	"	100th	"	Boys' Gate	7th "	"	110th	"	Warriors' Gate

CENTRAL PARK.

Central Park is the great pleasure ground of New York, and the chief point of interest for visitors. If the stranger with but half a day at command fails to visit it, he misses the great "show place" of the city. Any city can show its streets, hotels, theaters and churches. Few can exhibit such rural charms, adorned by art in the midst of its streets and houses. Eight hundred and forty-three acres of lawn, drives, shady walk, garden and wood, lake and brook, right in the heart of the town. At once a sanitary measure, play ground for children, grand avenues for lordly carriages and whispering places for lovers. The wilderness of marsh, rough hill and tangled woodland, extending from 59th to 110th streets, between 5th and 8th Avenues, was taken in hand by the engineer and landscape gardener in 1853, and even to-day it is not finished, though millions of money have been spent in the best investment New York ever made. There are two ways of seeing Central Park, afoot or with a horse. Neither will show the whole, as the drives miss much of the finer and more elaborate features of the places, and the walks fail to give some of the best prospects and out-looks. More than this, many points of interest are not in reach of carriage or foot path, but must be seen from a boat. There are 15 miles of carriage roads, 8 miles of bridle paths for horseback riders, and over 25 miles of walks.

Large and comfortable open carriages are provided at the Fifth and Eighth Avenue entrances, for all visitors who care to drive through the grounds. The fare for the entire trip up to Mount St. Vincent, at the northern end of the Park, and return is only 25 cents. By taking a return or transfer ticket, the visitor may leave the carriage at the end and may return from any point where he chooses to take another carriage. For instance, on leaving the Fifth Avenue gate, a transfer ticket is taken (without extra charge) and after spending an hour or more at the art galleries and flower gardens on Eighth Avenue, carriages may be taken and quite another road may be traversed to 59th street. Another good plan is to leave the carriage at the Terrace, cross the Lake and going through the Ramble, visit the Belvedere. Then walk along the breezy paths round the great Resevoirs to Mt. St. Vincent, where any carriage that passes may be taken back to the Eighth or Fifth Avenue entrances. Another pleasant trip is to walk to the Terrace and then take a carriage for

Mt. St. Vincent. From this place a rather longer, but exceedingly pictruesque walk, may be taken through the woods and up the lovely valley that leads off to the west towards Eighth Avenue and then through the pine woods to the Belvedere and the Ramble. Crossing the Lake again another carriage may be taken at the Terrace for home. The simple ride up and back, a distance of about five miles, shows many of the chief points of interest in the Park and gives a most charming journey. All the grand turnouts and carriages may be seen on the road and stops are made at such places as offer good views of the various statues and prospects. From three o'clock till dark is the best time to see the driving and the display of fine horses and gorgeous apparel. Saturday and Sunday are the most brilliant days of the week, but at any day or hour there will be much to see and enjoy. These Park carriages are under the control of the Park Commissioners and may be taken without hesitation as they are always safe and clean. Everybody uses them, and they are considered quite as elegant as the public hacks that may be hired at the gates. These hacks and open carriages charge 50 cents or more for each passenger and only hold four. The visitors who prefer them, will find plenty at each entrance, but sensible people go in the cheaper and more democratic Park carriages.

The Bridle Roads.

These roads are marked "for visitors on horseback only," and are exclusively devoted to their use. They join the drives near the gates and pass through some very retired and interesting parts of the Park. A good galop may be obtained upon them without fear, as they avoid the greater part of the drives and go under or over nearly all the foot-paths.

The Park Afoot.

This is, by far, the best way to see Central Park. The visitor who has only a short time to give to the place, and who wishes to "do all the sights" as easily and conveniently as possible, had best take a Seventh Avenue car and enter at the "Artisan's Gate" at the end of Seventh Avenue on 59th street. On entering, the broad path may be taken that gently curves to the right, and passes under a pretty vine-covered bridge. The bridges in the Park are all of great interest and beauty. No two are alike. Each is a study in itself, and it is well worth the while to notice them. Beyond the bridge the path climbs a small hill and crosses an iron bridge over one of the bridle paths. Here we turn to the right and presently come to the great lawn

Play Ground.

Visitors are generally not allowed to walk on the grass, but on certain days this place is declared free and then thousands of boys and young children roam on this wide field and play ball and other games. On such days signs are put up marked, "Common," and then the grass land is free. Off to the left here may be seen a mass of high bare rock. Such places as this, where there is no grass, are always free everywhere in the Park. Going on we pass through a rustic arbor and come to the

Carousel.

Here are swings, a "merry-go-round," and plenty of amusement for the younger children. Leaving these delights, we turn sharply to the right and go under another bridge and come to a high rock bank surmounted by an immese rustic arbor. This is one of the sights of the Park, and it is well worth while to turn aside and climb over the smooth rocks to see it. Coming back to the path we soon come to

The Dairy.

This is a restaurant where milk and ice-cream and a few simple things are for sale, and it furnishes a nice place for children's lunches. Swings and other amusements are provided near by. Just before reaching the Dairy the path turns to the right and soon comes to

The Marble Arch.

This is an archway under the road, with steps leading up to the paths beyond. The archway and stairs are all of marble, and the structure is both massive and beautiful. Mounting the steps we come suddenly upon one of the grand sights of the Park. Here the drive divides and we enter

The Mall.

This a broad path lined with trees and extending from the Marble Arch to the Terrace. It gives a fine view of this part of the Park and makes the grand promenade. The Belvedere tower can be seen at the end of the long vista, and here may be seen all gay driving and the crowds of pleasure-seekers, on their way to the lake and the rambles. The famous goat carriages, for infant rides, are here also. Three of the best statues in the Park may been seen here. The statute of Shakspeare, a standing figure, comes first. Next is the figure of Walter Scott; and a short distance to the left is a fine figure of an Indian hunter and his dog. Farther off to the left may be seen the large level field known as

The Common.

A flock of sheep roam over the grass, tended by a gray old shepherd and a very knowing shepherd dog, whose actions in his care of the flock afford amusement and study for all interested in such matters. Instead of taking the Mall and going directly to the Lake we may here take the first or second path to the right. Passing under the road we follow the winding path down hill and under another stone bridge to

The Museum and Menagerie.

Here a collection of birds and wild animals of various kinds and a museum of natural history is opened free, and an hour or more may be profitably spent in examining both. The objects are all close together, and it requires no special guidance to find them all. Having seen these things take the same path back as far as the place where it divides just under three great willow trees. Keeping on we pass another small play-ground for children, and keeping off to the left soon come to a part of the drive. Crossing the road-way and taking the path to the right, and then keeping off in that direction, we come to a few stone steps and then enter a long rustic arbor at the

Great Circle.

Here many of the pleasure riders turn in, and driving round view the prospect or stop at the pretty stone cottage for lunch. From the arbor there is a view on one side down over the Mall, where the bands play, and over the terrace and the drive. The stone cottage to the right is

The Casino.

It is a lunch room or restaurant, and is much patronized by the visitors who come in carriages. Walking through the arbor we may go down the steps and come out on

The Terrace.

This is the most striking and remarkable feature of the park. It is of a fine soft stone and covered with the most beautiful carvings. The central stairway goes down under the road, and the two side stairways are beyond the road. The three flights of stairs all meet below on the edge of the lake at the great bronze fountain. Going down the central stairs we enter an arched hall devoted to a restaurant. The walls are beautifully decorated with colored tiles, and it makes a cool and pleasant spot for a cream lunch. The other stairways show the outside of the terrace, and give one an opportunity to examine the figures of birds and animals carved in the stone walls and massive balustrade. Passing the fountain below, we come to the boat landing on

The Lake.

This irregular body of water cannot be all seen at once from any one spot, and the best way to examine it is to take a boat ride. The trip takes about half an hour and is very enjoyable. There are two classes of boats, one at a low price for all who choose to go with the general company, the other boats may be hired singly for a little larger fee. The prices are placarded on the boat house, and if the visitor has time it is well worth while to take the trip. From this point we may continue our walk by taking the path to the right of the boat landing and following the shore of the lake. We soon come to a fine iron bridge over the lake, and from the top get a good view of the lake and the beautiful shores on both sides. The swans and other birds also make a feature of interest. The shelving shore at the left of the bridge is known as "The Beach," and is a favorite place of resort in warm weather. Crossing the bridge we enter the most interesting part of the whole Park, and known as

The Ramble.

This, as its name implies, is a place where one may ramble for hours through shady paths, through mossy dells, over picturesque bridges, along winding lanes, among deep thickets, past bold rocks, and through woods and scattered grass. The paths, both small and great, wander in every conceivable direction, and cross each other in such a delightfully confusing way that there is no end of amusement in following them to see where they really do go. Arbors and seats are placed everywhere, and pretty views come as surprises everywhere. By taking the broad path from the bridge, a little to the left, we soon come to the donkey stand, where the children may indulge in a donkey ride if they are so inclined. Following the shore of the Lake we soon cross a rustic bridge, and mounting some steps come to

The Schiller Monument.

This is a portrait bust, and is said to be a fine work of art. Turning to the right we follow the signs pointing the way to

The Cave.

This is found in a deep rocky dell, and is worth visiting for the sake of the picturesque views it affords at both entrances and for the solemn company of owls sitting inside. Passing through the Cave we may climb the steep steps beyond, and take the path over head, or we may return by the way we came. If we return the path may be taken to the left and soon after to the right. This leads to a broad path up the hill to the right again. At the next turn go to the left, and the path will lead us up over the rocks to the top of the hill where stands

The Belvedere.

This is a stone tower or out-look giving an extensive view over the park and the country road about. To the south may be seen the spires of the lower part of the city. To the west is the Hudson and the country beyond. East of the East River some of the Islands, Harlem, and the Long Island shore. To the north lies the two great reservoirs, and beyond there is the upper part of the city, with a glimpse of High Bridge. At the foot of the tower on the east side the path round the reservoirs may be taken through a pretty valley of hedges. A few steps beyond to the right is a flight of stone steps leading down into the Ramble again. No particular directions need be given here. The visitor may wander where he likes, look at the rabbits, peacocks and other birds, and easily find his own way back to the lake. Crossing by the Bridge we may take the path along the beach, and go part way round the Lake to the right. Meeting the drive again, we come to the statue of "the Falconer," placed on a high rocky bank. Here the path along the road-side may be taken to the left, and presently we come to the Common again. Here is a bronze group of eagles, and another path leading past there to the Mall. Another path to the right leads to the little soda fountain stand called

The Springs.

From this part we may keep off to the right, and by going round the Common come out the 8th Avenue entrance on 59th street. By returning to the Mall we may keep on down the drive-way to the left, or to Fifth Avenue and 59th street. At the end of the Mall, near the Marble Arch, the paths to the right along the road-way lead to Sixth and Seventh Avenues. The path on the right hand side leads to Seventh Avenue, and the path on the left of the road goes to Sixth Avenue. This walk does not by any means include all the Park. It has shown all the chief points of interest within easy reach, and placed them in such an order as to enable the stranger to see as much as possible in a short time.

Other Parks.

Besides Central Park, New York has a number of smaller parks or squares. The Battery, at the foot of Broadway, is the oldest and most famous. Bowling Green is close to it, and is also another relic of revolutionary times. City Hall Park and Union and Madison Squares have each been described under the head of "Broadway." Washington Square is bounded by Waverley Place, Macdougal, Fourth, and Wooster streets, and is ornamented with trees, lawns, and a fountain. Tompkins Square is between Avenues A and B, joining Tenth and Seventh streets. Stuyvesant Square was formerly a part of the old Peter Stuyvesant farm, and was a gift to the city. It is bounded by Rutherford and Stuyvesant Places, and E. 15th and E. 17th streets, while second Avenue crosses it from north to south. Gramercy Park is a private park, on Third and Fourth Avenues, between E. 20th and E. 21st streets. Reservoir Park is on Sixth Avenue, and is described under that Avenue. Besides these are Hamilton Square, situated between

Third and FourthAvenues, near 66th and 67th streets. Bloomingdale Square, between Eighth and Sixth Avenues and W. 53d and 57th streets. Manhattan Square, on the same avenues between W. 77th and 81st streets. Mount Morris Square, in Harlem, is one of the most attractive and picturesque of the smaller squares; it is between 120th and 124th streets, on Fifth Avenue.

Excursions Round About.

the vicinity of New York presents attractions in every direction and in the greatest variety. Not only are the two large cities of Brooklyn and Jersey City within easy reach, but by the sea shore, along the two rivers, and in the country beyond are many places worth visiting. All the most popular places of resort are connected with the city by boat or rail, and the excursions thus offered are both cheap and plentiful. The first, and perhaps the best, are by the sea shore. Long Branch, the fashionable sea-side resort, is within easy reach by boat or rail from Jersey City. By boat the visitor lands at Sandy Hook, and affording views of the Highlands of New Jersey, a short rail ride by the beach. Coney Island and Rockaway Beaches are nearer, and are both reached by boats, and each presents good surf bathing and all the usual delights of a very democratic watering-place. Staten Island, still nearer the city, may be reached by boat in half an hour. Boats touching at places on the east side of the Island take one quite near the Narrows and within easy walking of the forts and heights. Boats for the north side of the Island go through the long inlet known as the Kills, and passing a number of pretty villages enter Raritan Bay, affording some charming views of the Jersey shore and Orange mountains. Another line of boats run farther on to Perth Amboy, and making a still more extended excursion. Other excursions may be made to Flushing, Jamaica, Babylon, and other points on Long Island by rail and ferry. Boat excursions may be made on both the East and North River. Boats to Harlem leave every half hour from down-town piers, and passing up East river skirt the eastern side of the city, pass Blackwell's, Ward's, and Randall's Islands, each with their public and charitable institutions, and entering Harlem river, stop near the Third Avenue bridge. Here other boats may be taken for High Bridge. This famous place of resort is noted for its great stone bridge carrying the Croton water pipes over the deep valley, and its picturesque scenery. High Bridge may also be reached by rail from the Grand Central Depot. From High Bridge the cars may be taken up the Harlem River valley to Spuyten Duyvil on the Hudson. The ride from this point down the river to 34th street gives a fine view of the Hudson and the Palisades, and passes the villages of Mount Washington, Carmansville, and Manhattanville, and the west side of the city, of which they form a part. Boats on the Hudson give excursions of varying length, from the little half-hour trip to Fort Lee to the all-day trip to Albany. Yonkers, Tarrytown, and West Point may all be visited by boat or rail within ten hours. No more romantic and beautiful river scenery can be found in this country than on the Hudson, and the visitor should go up as far as West Point, even if he neglects everything else. The Hudson is New York's great natural show piece, and if one is visited the other should be. Even in winter there is much to see from the car window, as the railroad clings to the shore the entire distance.

The Cemeteries.

There are eight great cemeteries near New York, and each is finely laid out and profusely ornamented with monuments. Greenwood is located on Gowanus Heights, Brooklyn, and is easily reached by horse cars from South Ferry or Hamilton Ferry. The Cemetery of the Evergreens is also in Brooklyn, and may be reached by horse cars from Atlantic, Fulton, and South 7th street ferries. Cypress Hills is just beyond the Evergreens and is reached by cars from Fulton, South, and Williamsburg ferries. Woodlawn is near Fordham, on the line of the Harlem Railroad, and is reached by that line. New York Bay Cemetery is on the west shore of the Bay, two miles an a half beyond Jersey City. It may be reached by road or horse cars, or by boat in summer. Calvary Cemetery is at Newtown, L. I., about two miles and a half from the 10th street ferry. This is the chief Catholic cemetery of the city. Trinity Church Cemetery is located between 153d and 154th streets. To reach it, cars on the Hudson River railroad for Carmansville station from 34th street station or by the Boulevard omnibusses. Mount Olivet Cemetery is at Maspeth, L. I., some three miles and a half from Grand and Houston street ferries. In addition to these are a number of minor cemeteries of less importance. Below is a full list.

CALVARY.—Office, 266 Mulberry st., N. Y. Located near Newtown. Long Island, 2½ miles from 10th st. ferry. Reached by Grand st, and Newtown Railroad.

CITY.—Office, E. 11th st. cor. Third avenue, N. Y. On Hart's Island. By ferry from foot E. 110th st.

CYPRESS HILL.—Offices, 124 Bowery and 744 Broadway, N. Y. Grounds on Myrtle avenue and Jamaica plank road, 5 miles from Williamsburg ferries. Reached by cars from Fulton ferry.

EVERGREENS.—Office at Cemetery. Grounds are 3 miles east of Brooklyn, L. I., on the Bushwick road. Cars from Fulton ferry.

GREENWOOD.—Office, 30 Broadway, N. Y. Grounds on Gowanus Heights, Brooklyn, L. I., 3 miles from Fulton and 2 miles from Hamilton avenue ferries. Reached by horse cars from both ferries.

LUTHERAN.—Office, 293 Broadway, N. Y. Grounds on the Jamaica turnpike, near Middle Village, L. I., 4 miles from the Williamsburg ferries. Reached by railroad from S. 7th st. ferry, Williamsburg.

MACHPELAH.—Office, 160 W. 24th st., N. Y. Located at New Durham, Hudson Co., N. J., 1 mile from Weehawken ferry, foot of W. 42d st.

MARBLE.—Office, 65 Second st., N. Y. Grounds in Second st., bet. First and Second avenues. Reached by the Second avenue cars.

MOUNT OLIVET.—Office, 67 Wall st., N. Y. Grounds near Maspeth, L. I., 3½ miles from Grand and Houston st. ferries. Reached by Metropolitan avenue cars, from S. 7th st. ferry, Williamsburg.

NEW YORK BAY.—Office, 5 Dey st., N. Y. Grounds on the west bank of New York Bay, 2½ miles below Jersey City. Reached by horse cars from the Jersey City ferry.

OAK HILL CEMETERY is on the west bank of the Hudson, near the village of Nyack, Rockland County, N. Y., 28 miles from N. Y. City.

POTTER'S FIELD.—New York. On Ward's Island.

POTTER'S FIELD.—Brooklyn, N. Y. Is at Flatbush, L. I.

TRINITY CHURCH.—Office, 187 Fulton st., N. Y. Grounds at 155th st. and Tenth avenue. Reached by Hudson River Railroad, 152d st.

UNION.—Office, 192 Rivington st., N. Y. Grounds near Wyckoff avenue, Brooklyn, L. I., 3½ miles from Division av. and Grand st. ferry.

WOODLAWN.—Office, 48 E. 23d st., N. Y. Situated in Westchester Co., 7 miles from Harlem Bridge. Reached by Harlem Railroad.

WASHINGTON CEMETERY, L. I. Reached by Hamilton ferry and Coney Island R. R.

CHURCHES OF NEW YORK.

Hours of Service. On the Sabbath: 10½ A.M., generally; P.M. in winter, 3½ and 4 in summer; evening, 7½. Week day evening services, usually Wednesday, 7½ o'clock.

M.—Morning services. A.—Afternoon services. E.—Evening services.

BAPTIST.

Abyssinian (col'd), 166 Waverley place; M. and E.
Amity, W. 54th street, near Eighth av.; M. and A.
Antioch, 278 Bleecker street.
Berean, 35 Downing street; M. and E.
Bethany Chapel, W. 81st cor. 11th av.
Calvary, 50 W. 23d st.; Rev. R. S. McArthur.
Central, 220 W. 42d st.
Central Park, E. 83d st., near Second av.
East, Madison st., cor. Gouverneur.
Ebenezer, 154 W. 36th st.
Fifth avenue, W, 46th st., n. Fifth av.; Rev. Thomas Armitage, D.D. M. and A.
First, Park av., cor. E. 39th st.; Rev. Thomas D. Anderson, D.D. M. and A.
First German, E. 14th st., near First av.
First, Harlem, Fifth av., cor. 126th st.
First Swedish.
First Mariner's, Oliver st., cor. Henry.
Free Will Baptist, 104 W. 17th st.
Grace, 405 W. 29th st.
Harlem Temple, 125th st., n. Fourth av.; M. and E.
Macdougal street, 24 Macdougal st.
Madison avenue, Madison av., cor. E. 31st st.; Rev. James F. Elder, D.D. M. and E.
North, 120 Christopher st.
Pilgrim, W. 33d st., n. Eighth av. M. and E.
Plymouth, 447 W. 51st st., n. Ninth av.
Second German. 453 W. 45th st.
Second, Harlem 111th st., bet. Third and Fourth avenues.
Sixth street, 644 Sixth st.
Sixteenth, 257 W. 16th st., n. Eighth av. M. and E.
South, 235 W. 25th st., n. Eighth av.; pastor, Rev. A. C. Osborn, D.D. M. and E.
Stanton street, 36 Stanton st. M. and E.
Tabernacle, 162 Second av. M. and E.
Trinity, E. 55th st., n. Lexington av. M. and E.
West 53d street, W. 53d st., n. Seventh av. M. and E.
Tabernacle Church Mission, 189 E. 20th st.
First Baptist Mission, Laight st., cor. Varick.
Bethesda Baptist Mission, 233 E. 33d st.
German Baptist Mission, 417 W. 43d st., n. Ninth av.
Second Baptist Mission, Grand st., cor. Clinton; Rev. Samuel Alman, 66 Rivington st.
Bethany Baptist Mission, cor. Boulevard and 86th st.
Zion (colored) Baptist, 7 Seventh av.
German Mission, Third av. n. 121st street.
Shiloh (colored), Third av., n. 126th street.

CONGREGATIONAL.

Tabernacle, Sixth av., cor. W. 34th st.; pastor, Rev. Wm. M. Taylor. M. and E.
Disciples, Madison av., cor. 45th st.; Rev. George H. Hepworth. M. and E.
Harlem, Second av., cor. 125th st.; Rev. S. H. Virgin.
Welsh, 206 E. Eleventh st.
Tabernacle Bethany Mission, Ninth av., cor. 36th st.
Mission, W. 50th st., n. Eighth av.
Alliance Chapel, 68th st., n. Broadway.

FRIENDS.

Meeting-house, E. 15th st., cor. Rutherford place.
Meeting-house (orthodox), E. 20th st., near Third av.
Meeting-house, 43 W. 27th st., n. Sixth av.
Mission (orthodox), 303 E. 41st st.
Mission (orthodox), 135 W. 30th st., n. Sixth av.

GREEK.

Greek Mission, 951 Second av.

JEWS.

Adaareth El, 135 E. 29th st.
Adath Israel, E. 57th st., n. First av.
Ahawath Chesed, Lexington av., cor. E. 56th st.
Anshi Emeth, E. Houston st., cor. Ridge.
Anshi Bikur Cholim, 127 Columbia st.
Beth Cholim, 232 W. 28th st.
Beth El, 817 Lexington av., cor. 63d st.
Beth Hamidrash, 78 Allen st.
Beth Hamidrash, 2d, 153 Chatham st.
Beth Israel Bikur Cholim, 56 Chrystie street.

Mount Sinai Hospital,

Lexington Avenue, between Sixty-sixth and Sixty-Seventh Streets.

Bikur Cholim, U-Kadischa, 63 Chrystie street.
Bnai Israel, 41 Stanton st.
Bnai Jeshurun, 145 W. 34th st.
Bnai Sholom, 630 5th st.
Chisuck Amuno, E. 54th st., near Third av.
Darech Amuno, New York University.
Emmanuel, 43d st., cor. Fifth av.
Poel Zedeck, W. 29th st., cor. Eighth av.
Rodeph Scholem, 8 Clinton st.
Shaari Berocho, 306 Sixth st.
Shaari Roch Mim, 146 Norfolk st.
Shaari Tephila, W. 44th st., near Sixth av.
Shaari Zedeck, 38 Henry st.
Shaaer Hashamoin, 91 Rivington st.
Shagnarai Tikva, Lexington av., near E. 87th st.
Shearith Israel, W. 19th st., n. Fifth av.
Shearith Israel, 114 Columbia st.
Synagogue, Third av., cor. 124th st.

LUTHERAN.

Trinity, Avenue B, cor. 9th st.
St. James', 216 E. 15th st.
St. John's, 81 Christopher st.
St. Luke's, W. 42d st., n. Eighth av.
St. Mark's, 323 Sixth st.
St. Matthew's, 354 Broome st., cor. Elizabeth.
Immanuel, E. 83d st.
Bethlehem, 492 Grand st.
St. Paul's, 226 Sixth av.; Rev. F. W. Geissenhainer, D.D.
St. Peter's, Lexington av., cor. 46th st.
Holy Trinity, 47 W. 21st st., n. Sixth av.
Immanuel, E. 87th st.
St. Paul's, W. 123d st., n. Seventh av.
Church of our Saviour (Norwegian), 56 Monroe st.
Gustavus Adolphus (Swedish), 153 E. 22d.
St. John's, E. 119th st., n. Third av.
Church of Christ, 648 Sixth st.; Rev. G. U. Wenner, 528 Fifth st.
St. Stephen's Mission, 361 Broome st.
Emigrant House Chapel, 16 State st.
Luther Chapel, 435 E. Houston st.
St. Andrew's, W. 50th st., n Seventh av.

METHODIST EPISCOPAL.

Sabbath services in all the Methodist churches Morning and Evening.

Alanson, 52 Norfolk st.
Allen street, 126 Allen st.
Bedford street, 28 Morton st.
Beekman Hill, 321 E. 50th, n. Second va.
Bethel ship, foot of Carlisle st.
Central, 58 Seventh av.
Cornell Memorial, E. 76th st., n. Second av.
Duane, 294 Hudson st.
Eighteenth street, 307 W. 18th.
Five Points Mission, 61 Park st.
Forsyth street, 10 Forsyth st.
Forty-fourth street, 461 W. 44th st.
Forty-third street, 253 W. 43d st.
Free Tabernacle, 248 W. 34th st.
German, 252 Second st.
German Mission, 346 W. 40th st.
Grace, 104th st., n. Ninth av.
Greene street, 59 Greene st.
Hedding, 337 E. 17th st.
Hope, 125th st., n. Sixth av.
Jane street, 13 Jane st.
John street, 44 John st.
Lexington avenue, Lexington av., c. 52d.
Perry street, 122 Perry street.
Rose Hill, 223 E. 27th st.
St. James', Madison av., cor. 126th st.
St. John's, 231 W. 53d st.
St. Luke's, W. 41st st., n. Sixth av.
St. Mark's (colored), 65 W. 35th st.
St. Paul's, Fourth av., cor. 22d st.
Second avenue, Second av., cor. 119th st.
Second street, 276 Second st.
Seventh street, 24 Seventh st.
South Harlem, 111th st., n. Lexington av
Thirtieth street, 331 W. 30th st.
Thirty-fifth street, n. Tenth av.
Thirty-seventh street, 223 E. 37th st.
Twenty-fourth street, 359 W. 24th st.
Washington square, 137 W. 4th st.
Washington Heights.
Willett street, 7 Willett st.
Yorkville, E. 86th st., n. Fourth av.
Mission, 647 E. 16th st.
" Broadway, cor. 69th st.
Sixty-first street, 61st st., n. Third av.
Mission, 197 Mott st.
" 186 Franklin st.
Eleventh street Chapel, 545 E. 11th st., n. Avenue B.
German Mission, Pearl st., cor. Madison st.
Willett Mission, Cannon st., n. Broome.
German Mission, 98 Eighth st., n. First av.
Emanuel Mission (colored), 87 Attorney st.
Wesley Mission, 292 Stanton st., cor. Cannon.

AFRICAN METHODIST EPISCOPAL.

African Union, 161 W. 15th st.
Bethel, 214 Sullivan st.
Zion, 331 Bleecker st.
African Union, 132 W. 30th st.
Little Zion, E. 117th st., n. Fourth av.
Bethel Mission, 106 W. 30th st.

FREE METHODIST.

Free Methodist, 329 W. 37th st.

CALVINISTIC METHODIST.

Welsh, 225 E. 13th st.

Deaf and Dumb Institute.

MORAVIAN.

Moravian Church, Lexington av., cor. E. 30th st.
Moravian Mission, 636 Sixth st.

PRESBYTERIAN.

Allen street, 61 Allen st., n. Grand. M. and A.
Brick, Fifth av., cor. 37th st., M. and A.
Canal street, Greene st., n. Canal.
Central, W. 56th st., n. Broadway. M. and E.
Covenant, Park av., cor. E. 35th st.; pastor, Rev. M. R. Vincent, D.D. M. and A.
Covenant (colored), Prince st., cor. Sullivan st.
Eighty-fourth street, W. 84th, st., n. Boulevard; Rev. W. W. Newell, D.D.
Fifth avenue, Fifth av., cor. W. 55th st.; Rev. John Hall, D.D. M. and A.
First, Fifth av., cor W. 11th st.; Rev. William M. Paxton, D.D. M. and A.
Fourth avenue, 286 Fourth av., cor. E. 22d st.; Rev. Howard Crosby, D.D. M. and E.
Fourteenth street, E. 14th st., cor. Second av. M. and E.
Fourth, W. 34th st., n. Sixth av. M. and A.
French Evangelical, 9 University place.
German, 290 Madison st.
Harlem, E. 125th st., n. Fifth av.
Madison square, Madison av., cor. E. 24th st.; Rev. W. J. Tucker, D.D. M. and A.
Manhattanville, Ninth av., cor. 126th st.
Memorial, Madison av., cor. 53d st.; Rev. C. S. Robinson, D.D. M. and E.
Mount Washington, Inwood.
Murray Hill, E. 40th st., n. Lexington av. M. and E.
New York, 167 W. 11th st.
North, Ninth av., c. W. 31st st. M. and E.
Phillips, E. 73d st., c. Madison av.; Rev. Samuel D. Alexander, D.D. M. and A.
Puritans, W. 130th st., n. 5th av., pastor emeritus; Rev. Geo. B. Cheever D.D.; pastor, Rev. Edward L. Clark.
Rutgers, Madison av., cor. E. 29th st.; Rev. N. W. Conkling, D.D. M. and E.
Scotch, 53 W. 14th street, n. Sixth av. M. and A.
Sea and Land, Market st., cor. Henry. M. and E.
Seventh, Broome st., cor. Ridge. M. and E.
Shiloh (colored), 140 Sixth av. and 135 W. 30th st.; Rev. H. H. Garnet, D.D.
Spring street, 246 Spring st., n. Varick. M. and A.
Thirteenth street, 145 W. 13th st.; Rev. Samuel D. Burchard, D.D. M and E.
University place, University place, cor 10th st.; Rev. Robert R. Booth, D D. M. and A.
Washington Heights, 155th st., cor Boulevard; Rev. Charles A. Stoddard, D.D.
West, W. 42d st., n. Fifth av.; Rev. Thomas S. Hastings, D.D. M. and E.
Westminster, 151 W. 22d st., n. Seventh av.
West Twenty-third street, W. 23d st., n. Seventh av.; Rev. Erskine N. White, D.D. M. and E.
First Union, Yorkville, 145 E. 86th st.
Chapel of Brick Church, 228 W. 37th st., n. Seventh av.
Chapel of Fifth av. Church, 127 Seventh av.
Alexander Chapel of Fifth av. Church, 7 and 9 King st.
Mission of Fifth av. Church, 416 E. 14th st., n. First av.
Chapel of First Church, 35 W. 12th st.
Mission of W. Twenty-third street Church, 273 W. 25th st.
Chapel of University-place Church, 167 W. 11th st.
Emmanuel Chapel of University-place Church, Sixth st., near Avenue D.
Memorial Chapel of Madison square Church, E. 30th st., near Third av.
German Mission of Madison square Church. 206 E. 31st st.
Grace Chapel of Fourth avenue Church, 340 E. 23d st., near First av.
Chinese Mission of Fourth avenue Church, 523 Pearl st.
Hope Mission of Fourth avenue Church, Avenue C, cor. Fourth st.
Faith Chapel of West Church, 419 W. 46th st., near Ninth av.
Memorial Chapel of Covenant Church, 306 E. 42d, near Second av.
Mission of 14th street Church, E. 12th, near Avenue B.
Mission of Seventh Church, 203 Rivington st.
Krebs Mission (colored), 59 Thompson st.
Salem Mission of Scotch Church, 185 Spring st.
Immanuel Mission of Scotch Church, 54 W. 15th st.
Westside Chapel of Fourth Presbyterian Church, 439 W. 33d st.
Bethesda Mission of Rutgers Presbyterian Church, 336 W. 29th

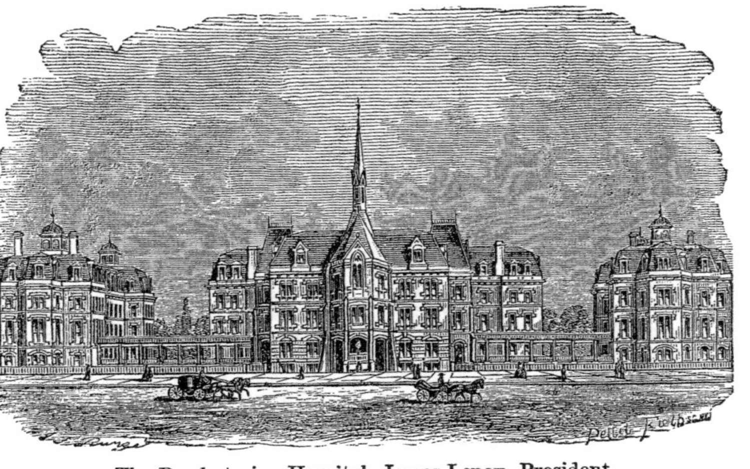

The Presbyterian Hospital, James Lenox, President,

Madison and Fourth Avenues, and Seventieth and Seventy-first Streets.

Goodwill Mission of Memorial Church, Second av., cor. 52d st.
Mission of Central Church.
Mission of Murray Hill Church, 30 Stuyvesant st.

UNITED PRESBYTERIAN.

Eleventh street, 206 E. 11th st.
Jane street, 41 Jane st.
Seventh avenue, 29 Seventh av.
Seventh, 434 W. 44th st.
Third, 41 Charles.
West Twenty-fifth street, 161 W. 25th st.
Harlem, E. 127th st., near Third av.
Charles street Mission, Eighth av., cor. W. 34th st.
Mission, Third av., cor. 86th st.
Harlem, E. 116th, bet. Second and Third avs.

REFORMED PRESBYTERIAN.

First, 123 W. 12th st.
First, 426 W. 28th st.
Second, 221 W. 39th st., near Seventh av.
Third, 238 W. 23d st.
Fourth, 365 W. 48th st., near Ninth av.
Mission, 440 W. 40th st.

PROTESTANT EPISCOPAL.

All Angels', W. 81st st., near Eleventh av.
All Saints', 286 Henry st.
Annunciation, 142 W. 14th st.
Anthon Memorial, 139 W. 48th st., near Seventh av. M. and E.
Ascension, Fifth av., cor. Tenth st.; Rev. John Cotton Smith, D.D. M. and A.
Atonement, Madison av., cor. 28th st.; rector, Rev. C. C. Tiffany. M. and E.
Beloved Disciple, Madison av., cor. 89th st.
Calvary, Fourth av., cor. E. 21st st.; Rev. E. A. Washburn, D.D. M. and A.
Chapel of Holy Comforter, 365 West st.
Chapel of our Saviour, foot of Pike st., E. R.
Christ, Fifth av., cor. 35th st.
Du St. Esprit, 30 W. 22d st. M. and E.
Epiphany, 228 E. 50th st.
Grace, 800 Broadway; Rev. H. C. Potter, D.D.
Grace, E. 116th st., near Second av.
Heavenly Rest, Fifth av., near E. 45th st.; Rev. R. S. Howland, D.D.
Holy Apostles', Ninth av., cor. W. 28th st.
Holy Communion, Sixth av., cor. 20th st.
Holy Martyrs', 39 Forsyth st.
Holy Saviour, E. 25th st., near Madison av.; rector, Rev. A. B. Carter, D.D.
Holy Sepulchre, E. 74th st., near Fourth av.
Holy Trinity, Madison av., cor. E. 42d st.; Rev. Stephen H. Tyng, Jr., D.D. M. and A. in summer, M. and E. in winter.
Holy Trinity of Harlem, Fifth av., cor. 125th st.
Incarnation, Madison av., cor. 35th st.; Rev. Arthur Brooks. M. and E.
Intercession, 158th st., cor. Eleventh av.
Mediator, Eleventh av., near 51st st. M. and E.
Nativity, 70 Avenue C.
Redeemer, E. 82d st., cor. Fourth av.
Resurrection, E. 85th st., near Third av.
Santigo, 30 W. 22d st.
St. Alban's, E. 47th st., n. Lexington av
St. Ambrose, 117 Thompson st.
St. Andrew's, 127th st., near Fourth av.; Rev. G. B. Draper, D.D.
St. Ann's 7 W. 18th st.; Rev. Thomas Gallaudet, D.D.
St. Bartholomew's Madison av., cor. 44th st.; Rev. Samuel Cooke, D.D.
St. George's, Rutherford place, cor. E. 16th st.; Rev. Stephen H. Tyng, D. D. M. and A.
St. Clement's, 108 Amity st.; Rev. Theodore A. Eaton, D.D. M. and E.
St. Ignatius, W. 40th st., near Sixth av.; Rev. F. C. Ewer, D.D.
St. James', E. 72d st. near Third av.
St. John Baptist, 261 Lexington av.; Rev. C. R. Duffie, D.D. M. and A., winter M. and E.
St. John Evangelist, 222 W. 11th st. M. and E.
St. John's, 46 Varick st.; Rev. S. H. Weston, D.D. M. and A.
St. Luke's, 483 Hudson st.; Rev. I. H. Tuttle, D.D. M. and A.
St. Mark's, Stuyvesant st., cor. Second av.; Rev. J. H. Rylance, D.D. M. and E.
St. Mary's, 128th st., near Tenth av.
St. Mary's, 45th st., near Seventh av.
St. Michael's, Broadway, cor. 99th st.; Rev. T. M. C. Peters, D.D.
St. Paul's, Broadway, cor. Vesey st; Rev. B. I. Haight, D.D. M. and E.
St. Peter's, 340 W. 20th st.; Rev. Alfred B. Beach, D.D. M. and A.
St. Philip's (colored), 305 Mulberry
St. Stephen's, 58 W. 46th st., near Sixth av. M. and E.
St. Thomas', Fifth av., cor. 53d st.; Rev. W. F. Morgan, D.D. M. and A.
St. Timothy, W. 57th st., near Eighth av.; Rev. G. J. Geer, D.D. M. and E.
Transfiguration, E. 29th st., near Fifth av.; Rev. G. H. Houghton, D.D. M. and A.
Trinity, Broadway, opp. Wall st.; Rev. Morgan Dix, D.D. M. and A.

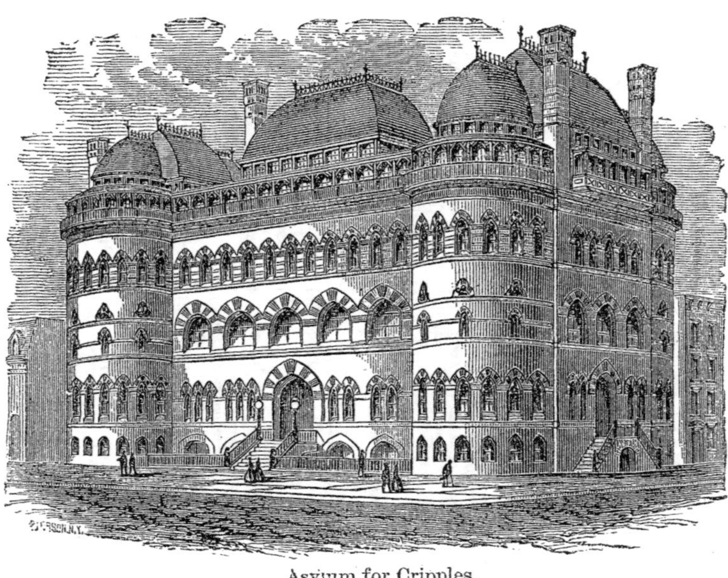

Asylum for Cripples.

Trinity Chapel, 15 W. 25th st.; Rev. C. E. Swope, D.D. M. and A.
Zion, Madison av., cor. 38th st.; Rev. J. N. Gallaher. M. and A.
Calvary Chapel, 218 E. 23d st.
Rutgers street Mission, 58 Rutgers st.
St. George's Mission, Chapel of Free Grace, 408 E. 19th st.
St. George's Mission, German, 420 E. 14th st.
St. George's Mission, Chapel of Bread of Life, 420 E. 14th st.
St. Mark's Mission, 141 Avenue A.
Ascension Chapel of Shepherd's Flock, 330 W. 43d st.
Ascension Chapel of Comforter, Greenwich st., cor. Jane.
Mission Chapel of St. Thomas' Church, E. 60th st., near Second av.
Atonement Chapel, 418 W. 41st st.
Grace Chapel, E. 14th st., near Third av.
St. Chrysostom Chapel, Seventh av., cor. 39th st.
St. Augustine Chapel, 264 Bowery
Incarnation Chapel of Reconciliation, 242 E. 31st st.
Bethlehem Mission, Ninth av., cor. 33d st.
St. Barnabas Chapel, 306 Mulberry st.
Mission Chapel, 130 Stanton.
French, Fourth av., near 21st st.
Italian, in St. Ambrose Church, 117 Thompson st. and 46 Franklin st.
Italian, 508 Pearl st.

REFORMED EPISCOPAL.

First Reformed Episcopal, Madison av., cor. 47th st.; Rev. W. T. Sabine.
Second Reformed Episcopal, W. 26th st., near Seventh av.

REFORMED.

Bloomingdale, W. 71st st., near Ninth av.
Collegiate, Lafayette pl., cor. Fourth st.; Rev. Talbot W. Chambers, D.D. M. and A.
Collegiate, Fifth av., cor. 29th st.; Rev. William Ormiston, D.D. M. and E.
Collegiate, Fifth av., cor. 48th st.; Rev. Thomas E. Vermilye, D.D., and James M. Ludlow, D.D. M. and E.
Fourth German Mission, 246 W. 40th st., n. Eighth av.
German Evangelical Mission, 141 E. Houston st.
German Reformed Protestant, 129 Norfolk st.
Harlem, Third av., cor. 121st.; Rev. G. H. Mandeville, D.D.
Holland, W. 29th st., n Ninth av.
Madison av., Madison av., cor. 57th st.
Prospect Hill, E. 85th st., n Second av.; Rev. D. M. L. Quackinbush, D.D. M. and A.
South Fifth av., cor. 21st st.; Rev. E. P. Rogers, D.D. M. and A.
Thirty-fourth st., 307 W. 34th st. M. and E.
Union, 25 Sixth av. M. and E.
Washington Heights, Wash'n Heights.
Collegiate Mission, 160 W. 29th st. M. and E.
Collegiate Mission, 514 Ninth av., n. 39th st.
Collegiate Mission, Seventh av., cor. 54th st. M. and E.
Collegiate Mission, Fulton st., n. William; Rev. George J. Mingins.
South Church Mission Chapel, 348 W. 26th st.
Thirty-fourth street Church Mission, 405 W. 29th st.
German Evangelical Mission, 71 Av. B, cor. Fifth st.
German Evangelical Mission, Second av. N. W. cor. 52d st.

ROMAN CATHOLIC.

Annunciation, W. 131st st., n. Broadway.
Assumption, W. 49th st., n. Ninth av.
Epiphany, Second av., n. 22d st.
Holy Cross, 335 W. 43d st.
Holy Innocents, W. 37th st., n. Broadway.
Holy Name of Jesus, Broadway, n. 97th st.
Immaculate Conception, 505 E. 14th st.
Most Holy Redeemer, 165 Third st.
Nativity, 46 Second av.
Our Lady of Sorrow, 105 Pitt st.
St. Agnes, E. Forty-third st., n Third av.
St. Alphonso's, 10 Thompson st.
St. Andrew's, Duane st., cor. City Hall pl.
St. Ann's, 112 E. 12th st.; priest, Rev. T. S. Preston.
St. Anthony's, 143 Sullivan st.
St. Bernard's, 334 W. 14th st., n. Ninth av.
St. Boniface, E. 47th st., n. Second av.
St. Bridget's, Av. B, cor. Eighth st.
St. Cecilia, 105th st., bet. First and Second avs.
St. Colomba's, 339 W. 25th st.
St. Elizabeth, Broadway, cor. 187 st.
St. Francis, 139 W. 31st st.
St. Francis Xavier, 36 W. 16th st.
St. Gabriel's, E. 37th st., n. Second av.
St. James', 32 James st.; Rev. F. H. Farelly.
St. John Baptist, 209 W. 30th st.
St. John Evangelist, E. 50th st., n. Fifth av.
St. Joseph's, Sixth av., cor. W. Washington pl.

Institute for Blind.

St. Joseph's (German), W. 125th, n. Ninth av.
St. Lawrence, E. 84th st., n. Fourth av.
St. Mary's, 438 Grand st.
St. Mary Magdalen, E. 17th st.
St. Michael's, 407 W. 31st st.
St. Nicholas, 125 Second st.
St. Patrick's, Mott st., cor. Prince.
St. Paul's, W. 59th st., n. Ninth av.
St. Paul's, E. 117th st., n. Fourth av.
St. Peter's, Barclay st., cor. Church; Rev. M. J. O'Farrell.
St. Rose of Lima, 32 Canon st.
St. Stanislaus, 264 Madison av.
St. Stephen's, 149 E. 28th st.; Rev. E. McGlynn.
St. Theresa, Rutgers st., cor. Henry st.
St. Vincent de Paul, 127 W. 23d st.
St. Vincent, Lexington av., cor. 65th st.
Transfiguration, Mott st., cor. Park.

UNION OR UNDENOMINATIONAL CHURCHES AND MISSIONS.

Mariners' Church, cor. Madison and Catherine.
Port Society Mission.
Port Society Mission, Dover st. cor. Water.
Howard Mission, 40 New Bowery.
Wilson Mission, Av. A, cor. Eighth st.
Church of the Strangers, Neilson pl., (Mercer st.) n. Eighth st.; pastor, Rev. C. F. Deems, D.D.
Olivet Chapel, 62d st.; Rev. A. F. Schauffler.
Lebanon Chapel, 70 Columbia st.
Church of the Disciples, Madison av., cor. 45th st.; Rev. George H. Hepworth.
Carmel Chapel, 134 Bowery.
Rose Memorial Chapel, 418 W. 41st st.
Calvary Chapel, 153 Worth st.
De Witt Chapel, 135 Greenwich st.
Alliance Chapel, 68th st., n. Broadway.

UNITARIAN.

All Souls, Fourth av., cor. E. 20th st.; Rev. W. W. Bellows, D.D.
Messiah, Park av., cor. E. 34th st.
Third, Twenty-third st., n. Sixth av.; Rev. O. B. Frothingham.
Fourth, E. 128th st., n. Fourth av.
Mission, 30 Stuyvesant st., Plimpton Building.

UNIVERSALIST.

Third, 206 Bleecker st.; Rev. E. T. Sweetzer.
Fourth, Fifth av., cor. 45th st.; Rev. Edwin H. Chapin, D.D.
Our Saviour, W. 57th st., n. Eighth av.
Mission, 127th st., n. Fourth av.
Universalist Association, Sixth av., cor. 33d st.
Mission, Plimpton Building, 30 Stuyvesant st.
Mission, Brevoort Hotel, E. 54th st., n. Third av.

MISCELLANEOUS.

Christian Israelites, 108 First st.
German Evangelical Reformed, 97 Suffolk st.
Disciples, 24 W. 28th st.
German Evangelical, 138 W. 24th st. and 340 W. 53d st.
Catholic Apostolic, 128 W. 16th st.
Swedenborgian, 68 E. 35th st.
Messiah, Second Advent.
Welsh Church, 225 E. 13th st.
Second Advent, 68 East Broadway.
Second Advent, 405 Grand st.
Second Advent, Cooper Union, Room 24.
First Congregational Methodist, W. 24th st., n. Sixth av.
German Swedenborgian, 141 Christie st.
True Reformed Dutch, Perry st., cor. W. Fourth.
Mission, 435 E. Houston st.
Mission, 180 Wooster st.
Mission, Broadway, cor. 43d st.
Phelps' Mission, 330 E. 37th st.
Mission, W. 50th st., n. Eighth av.
Camp Mission, 116 Elizabeth st.
Mission, 116 Water st.
Mission, 405 W. 29th st.
Mission, 69 Ludlow st.
Mission, Third av., cor. 86th st.
Mission, Third av., n. 114th st.
Italian Mission, 99 South Fifth av.
Mission, 345 W. 28th st.
Star Mission, 169 W. 26th st., n. Seventh av.
Mission, Eighth av., cor. 34th st.
Mission, 454 W. 29th st.
Mission, Ninth av., cor. 36th st.
German Mission, W. 51st st., n. Tenth av.
German Mission, Eighth av., n. 68th st.
Mission, Essex st., n. Grand.

There are four societies of Spiritualists, four clubs of Free-Thinkers and Infidels, a company of Comte's followers, and other circles of a similar character, who advertise meetings weekly, in various halls throughout the city.

THE CHURCHES IN THE NEW TWENTY-THIRD AND TWENTY-FOURTH WARDS LATELY ADDED TO THE CITY.

BAPTIST.

Alexander av., cor. 141st st.; Rev. Wm. Marshall.

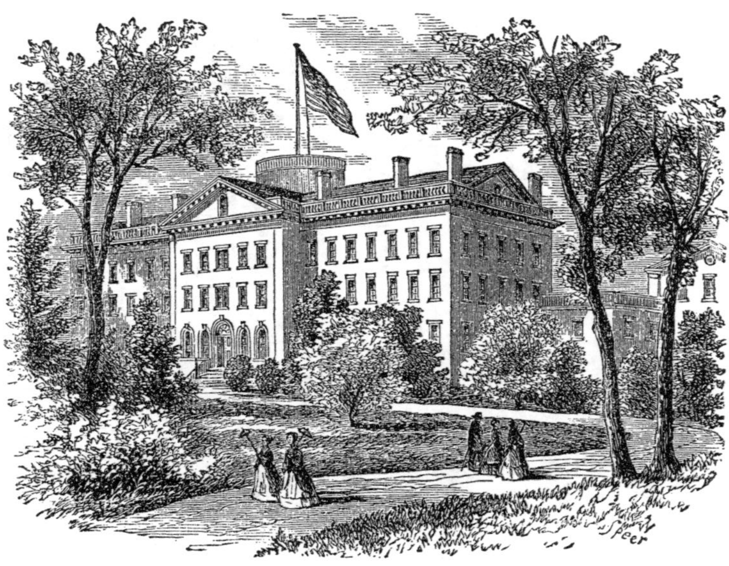

Bloomingdale Asylum for the Insane,

One Hundred and Seventeenth Street and Tenth and Eleventh Avenues.

Courtland av., n 158th st.; Rev. B. B. Gibbs.
Mount Hope, Monroe av.; Rev. J. B. Lewis.
Pilgrims, West Farms.
Bethel, German, Washington av., n. 168th st.; Rev. C. Geyer.
German Mission, Melrose.

CONGREGATIONAL.

Washington av., n 166th st.; Rev. J. L. Beaman.
Melrose.

LUTHERAN.

Courtland av., n 155th st.; Rev. Francis G. Zeumer, 154th st.
169th st., n Fulton av.

METHODIST.

Fordham; Rev. William Combs.
Mosholu; Rev. D. W. C. van Gaasbeck.
Washington av., n. 166th st.; Rev. J. P. Swift.
Washington av., n. 176th st.; Rev. T. Lamont.
West Farms.
Willis av., cor. 141 st.; Rev. Charles Hall, 141st st., n. Willis av.
158th st., n. Elton av.

PRESBYTERIAN.

Washington av., near 174th st.; Rev. George Nixon.
Washington av., near 167th st.; Rev. L. P. Cummings.
West Farms.
140th st., cor. Third av.; Rev. Gordon Mitchell.

PROTESTANT EPISCOPALIAN.

Alexander av., cor. 142d st.; Rev. C. S. Stephenson
Fordham; Rev. Mytton Mowry.
St. Ann's av., near 140th st.; Rev. W. Huckel
West Farms; Rev. Robert Scott
Third av., near 140th st.; Rev. Thomas R. Harris
166th st., near Boston av.; Rev. Albert S. Hull

REFORMED (DUTCH).

Fordham; Rev. Jacob Cole.
High Bridge; Rev. Hasbrouck Dubois.
Washington av., near 157th st.; Rev. G. Windemuth.
West Farms; Rev. John Simonson.
146th st., cor. Third av.; Rev. Hasbrouck Dubois.

ROMAN CATHOLIC.

150th st., near Third av.
Fordham.
170th st., near Franklin av.
Broadway, cor. 187th st.
Alexander av., cor. 137th st.
King's Bridge.
Washington av., near 176th st.

MISCELLANEOUS.

Disciples, 169th st., near Franklin av.

NEW YORK CITY MISSIONS.

135 Greenwich st.
153 Worth st.
70 Columbia st.
134 Bowery.
63 Second st.

MIDNIGHT MISSION.

Home, 260 Greene st.

MISSIONS AT THE FIVE POINTS.

Ladies' M. E. Mission, 61 Park st. Services every Sabbath at 3 P.M.
House of Industry, 155 Worth st. Services every Sabbath at 3 P.M.

HOWARD MISSION.

Howard Mission, 40 New Bowery. Services every Sabbath at 3 P.M.

CHURCHES FOR SEAMEN.

74 Madison st.
Oliver st., cor. Henry
Market st., cor. Henry.
Bethel, Pike st., East river.
Bethel, Pier 11, North river.
Bethel, 75 Beach st.
Dover st., cor. Water.
22 South st.
34 Pike st.
365 West st.

CHRISTIAN ASSOCIATIONS.

FOR YOUNG MEN AND YOUNG WOMEN.

Young Men's Christian Association Library and Reading-room, open daily, Fourth av., cor. 23d st.; Bowery Branch, 134 Bowery; Harlem Branch, Third av., cor. 122d st.; Yorkville Branch, Third av., cor. 86th st.
Ladies' Christian Home Association, Boarding-house for Young Women, 27 and 28 Washington sq.
Women's Library, 48 Bleecker st.
Churchman's Reading-rooms, 1255 Broadway.
German Young Men's Rooms, 141 E. Houston st.
Young Women's Christian Association, 7 E. 15th st.

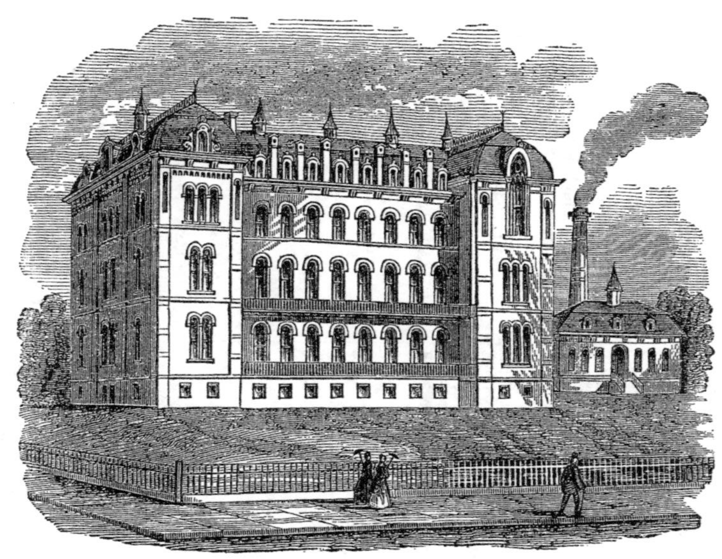

Woman's Hospital of the State of New York,

Forty-ninth and Fiftieth Streets, Lexington and Fourth Avenues.

COLLEGES AND SEMINARIES.

Academy of the Holy Cross, 343 W. 42d st.
Academy of the Sacred Heart, 49 W. 17th st.
Bellevue, E. 26th st. and First av.
Columbia College, Madison av. and E. 49th st.
College of the City of New York, Lexington av. and E. 23d st.
Eclectic, 223 E. 26th st.
General Theological Seminary of the Protestant Episcopal Church, W. 20th st. and Ninth av.
Hahnemann, 3 E. 53d st.
Homœopathic, Third av. and E. 23d st.
Home of the Evangelist, 52 Seventh st.
Hygeio Therapeutic, 95 Sixth av.
Manhattan, W. 131st st.
Medical College for Women, 187 Second av.
New York College of Dentistry, Broadway and 21st st.
New York Free Medical College for Women, 51 St. Mark's pl.
Pharmacy University, E. Washington sq.
Physicians and Surgeons, Fourth av. and E. 23d st.
Rutgers Female, 489 Fifth av.
St. Francis Xavier, 49 W. 15th st.
St. Louis, 232 W. 42d st.
University of the City of New York, 2 Washington sq.
University, E. 26th st. opp. Bellevue.
Union Theological Seminary, 9 University pl.
Veterinary, 205 Lexington ave.

CHARITABLE INSTITUTIONS.

DISPENSARIES.

Belleville Bureau for Relief of Out-Door Poor, foot of E. 26th st.
Central, 984 Eighth av.
Church of the Holy Communion, 328 Sixth av.
Church of the Holy Trinity, 44 E. 43d st.
Demilt, 401 Second av.
Eastern, 57 Essex st.
Eclectic, 223 E. 26th st.
For Women and Children, 128 Second av,
German, 65 St. Mark's pl.
German, West Side, 332 W. 40th st.
Harlem, 188 E. 122d st.
Hoffman, 158 W. 28th st.
Homœopathic, 59 Bond; 228 E. B'way; 45 W. 48th; Third av. c. E. 23d; 307 E. 55th; 578 Ninth av.
New York, Centre, c. White.
New York Ear, W. 36th st. and Ninth av.
New York Eye and Ear, 218 Second av.
N. Y. Free for Women, 51 St. Mark's pl.
New York Ophthalmic & Aural, 46 E. 12th
New York, for Children, 406 E. 15th st.
New York, for Diseases of the Skin, 101 E. 30th st.
New York, Tumor, 101 E. 30th st.
New York, for Cancer, and Hospital, 468 Sixth av.
New York, for Throat and Chest Diseases, 47 University pl.
New York Homœopathic, 483 Seventh av.
New York Orthopœdic, 126 E. 59th st.
North Eastern, 222 E. 59th st.
North Eastern Homœopathic, 307 E. 55th st.
Northern, Waverley pl., c. Christopher st.
North Western, Ninth av., c. W. 36th st.
Western, for Women and Children, 242 Ninth av.
Western Homœopathic, 413 W. 42d st.
Women's Institute, 30 W. 16th st.
Yorkville, 1482 Third av.
Yorkville Homœopathic, 162 E. 84th st.

HOMES, HOSPITALS, AND ASYLUMS.

Association for Befriending Children and Young Girls, 136 Second av.
Association for Improving the Condition of the Poor, Bible House.
Baptist Home for Aged, E. 68th st., Lexington av.
Bellevue Hospital, foot of E. 26th st.
Boarding Home for Women, 133 Macdougal st.
Boys' Lodging House, 128 Fulton st.
Bread and Beef House, 306 W. 52d st.
Chapin Home, 66th st. near Third av.
Children's Aid Society, 19 E. 4th st.
Children's Fold, 437 E. 58th st.
Children's Educational Relief Association, Office, 478 Grand st.
Christian Home for Women, 314 E. 15th st.
Colored Home, 65th st. near First av.
Colored Orphan Asylum, Boulevard, W. 143d st.
Commission of Emigration, Castle Garden
Day Nursery, 308 Mulberry st.
Day Nursery, 113 W. 20th st.
Dental Infirmary, 245 E. 23d st.
Emigrants' Refuge and Hospital, Castle Garden.

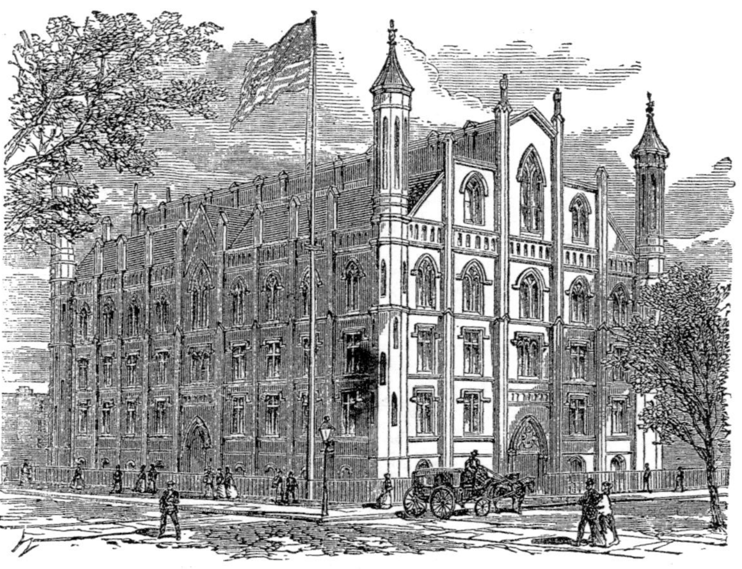

College of the City of New York,
Lexington Avenue, corner of Twenty-third Street.

Female Christian Home, 314 E. 15th st.
Five Points House of Industry, 155 Worth st.
Five Points Ladies' Mission, 61 Park st.
Foundling Asylum, E. 68th st., Third av.
Free Dormitory for Women, 54 W. 3d st.
Free Labor Bureau, 10 Clinton pl.
Free Training School for Women, 47 E. 10th st.
Friendly Society of St. Ambrose Church for the Relief of the Aged, 29 Charlton st.
German Hospital, 77th st. n. Fourth av.
Girls' Lodging House, 27 St. Mark's pl.
Guild of St. Catharine, 262 Bowery.
Hahnemann Hospital, 307 E. 55th st.
Hebrew Orphan Asylum, Third av. near 77th st.
Helping Hand Association, 160 W. 29th st.
Helping Hand for Men, 316 Water st.
Home for Old Men and Aged Couples, 487 Hudson.
Home for Aged and Infirm Deaf Mutes, 220 E. 13th.
Home for Aged and Infirm Israelites, 822 Lexington av.
Home for the Aged of the Church of the Holy Communion, 330 Sixth av.
Home for Friendless Girls, Seventh av. c. W. 13th st.
Home for Friendless Women, 86 W. 4th st.
Home for Incurables, Fordham.
Home for the Aged, 127 Cedar st.
Home for the Aged, 179 E. 70th st.
Home for the Blind, 219 W. 14th st.
Home for the Friendless, 32 E. 30th st.
Home for Respectable Aged and Indigent Females, 226 E. 20th st.
Home for Sailors' Children, Staten Island.
Boarding Home for Young Women, 27 Washington Square, N. Y.
House and School of Industry, 120 W. 16th st.
House of the Evangelists, 52 Seventh st.
House of the Good Shepherd, foot of E. 90th st.
House of the Good Shepherd, Rockland Co., 47 W. 25th st., N. Y.
House of Mercy (P. E.), W. 86th
House of Refuge, Randall's Island, 61 Bible House.
House of Rest for Consumptives, Tremont, 8 Wall.
Howard Mission, 40 New Bowery.
Infirmary for Women and Children, 128 Second av.
Institution for Improved Instruction of Deaf Mutes, 642 Seventh av.
Institution for the Blind, Ninth av. bet. 33d and 34th sts.
Institution for the Deaf and Dumb, 162d st., N. R.
Institution of Mercy (R. C.), 33 E. Houston st.
Institution of the Ladies' Union Aid Society of the M. E. Church, 255 W. 42d st.
Isaac Hopper Home, 110 Second av.
Isabella Heimath, Henry st., Astoria.
Ladies' Union Relief Association, Fifth av., 22d st.
Leake and Watts Orphan House, 112th st., Tenth av.
Lutheran Emigrant House, 16 State st.
Lying-in Asylum, 85 Marion st.
Magdalen Asylum, 88th st. near Fifth av.
Manhattan Eye and Ear Hospital, 233 E. 34th st.
Metropolitan Throat Hospital, 17 Stuyvesant st.
Midnight Mission, 260 Greene st.
Morgue, E. 26th st. and East River.
Mount Sinai Hospital, Lexington av., E. 66th st.
National Asylum for Disabled Soldiers, 171 B'way.
Newsboys' Lodging House, New Chambers st., William and Duane sts.
Newsboys' Home, 327 Rivington st.
North Eastern Homœopathic Dispensary, 307 E. 55th st.
Nursery, Child's Hospital and Lying-in Asylum, Lexington av. c. 51st st.
N. Y. Female Assistance Society, 34 E. 24th st.
N. Y. Society for the Prevention of Cruelty to Children, Office, 860 Broadway, c. 17th st.
N. Y. Homœopathic Medical College, Third av., E. 23d st.
N. Y. Hospital, 8 W. 16th st.
N. Y. Infant Asylum, 24 Clinton pl.
N. Y. Institute for the Relief of the Ruptured and Crippled, 42d st. and Lexington av.
N. Y. Juvenile Asylum, 61 W. 13th st.
N. Y. Medical College and Hospital for Women, c. 12th st. and Second av.
N. Y. Ophthalmic and Aural Institute, 46 E. 12th st.
N. Y. Ophthalmic Hospital, c. 23d st., Third av.
Orphan Asylum Society, 74th st. and Eleventh av.
Orphan Asylum of St. Vincent de Paul, 211 W. 39th
Orphan Home and Asylum of the P. E. Church, 49th st. between Fourth and Lexington avs.
Peabody Home, 33d st., Lexington av.
Presbyterian Home for Aged Christian Women, 73d st. near Madison av.

The Association for the Benefit of Colored Orphans,
Asylum, One Hundred and Forty-third Street and Tenth Avenue.

Presbyterian Hospital, 70th st. near Fourth av.
Protestant Half Orphan Asylum, 65 W. 10th st.
Roman Catholic Female Orphan Asylum, Madison av., 52d st.
Roman Catholic Male Orphan Asylum, 647 Fifth av.
Roman Catholic Orphan Asylum, Girls, 32 Prince st.
Roman Catholic Protectory, Fordham.
Roosevelt Hospital, Ninth av., 59th st.
Sailors' Home, 190 Cherry st.
Sailors' Snug Harbor, 74 Wall st.
Samaritan Home for the Aged, Ninth av. c. 14th st.
Seaman's Fund and Retreat, 12 Old Slip.
Shepherd's Fold, 86th st. c. Second av.
Shelter for Men, 316 Water st.
Shelter for Respectable Girls, 332 Sixth av.
Sheltering Arms, 129th st., Tenth av.
Sisters of the Stranger, 4 Winthrop pl.
Society for Relief of Poor Widows with Small Children, 143 Eighth st.
St. Augustine's Guild, 264 Bowery.
St. Barnabas' House, 304 Mulberry st.
St. Elizabeth's Hospital, 225 W. 31st st.
St. Francis' Hospital, 609 Fifth st.
St. John Baptist House, 220 Second av.
St. John's Guild, 52 Varick st.
St. Johnland, St. Luke's Hospital.
St. Joseph's Home for the Aged, 209 W. 15th st.
St. Joseph's Orphans, E. 89th st. c. Avenue A.
St. Luke's Home for Indigent Christian Females, 89th st. and Madison av.
St. Luke's Hospital, 54th st. and Fifth av.
St. Mary's Hospital for Children, 407 W. 34th st.
St. Stephen's Home, 145 E. 28th st.
St. Vincent's Home for Friendless Boys, 53 Warren st.
St. Vincent's Hospital, 195 W. 11th st.
Stranger's Rest, 510 Pearl st.
Throat and Chest Diseases, 47 University pl.
Trinity Chapel Home for Aged Women, 207 W. 27th st.
Union Home and School, 151st st. and Boulevard.
Water Street Mission and Home for Women, 273 Water st.
Wartburg Orphan's Home, Mt. Vernon.
Wilson Mission House and Home for Girls, 137 Avenue A, c. Eighth st.
Women's Aid Society and Home for Training Young Girls, 41 Seventh av.
Women's Hospital, 50th st. near Fourth av.
Working Women's Protective Union, 37 Bleecker st.
Women's Prison Association and the I. S. Hopper Home, 110 Tenth av.
Young Ladies' Christian Association, 7 E. 15th st.
Young Women's Aid Association, 85 E. 4th st.

HOTELS.

(E) means European Plan. (A) means American Plan. (A.E) means American and European plan.

Albemarle (E).....Broadway & 24th St.
Alborns (E)..............256 Fulton St.
Anson (E)................79 Spring St.
Anthony (E)............834 Broadway
Arlington (E)..........22 East 14th St.
Ashland (A) (E).....4th Av. & 24th St.
Astor (A) (E)............221 Broadway
Atlantic (A).......63 & 65 New Bowery
Belmont (E)..............137 Fulton St
Belvedere (A)....Irving place & 15th St
Bowery (E)................395 Bowery
Brandreth (E)....Broadway & Canal St.
Brevoort (E)...............11 Fifth Av.
Brevoort Place (E)....B'way & 10th St.
Broadway (A)..........B'way & 42d St.
Brower (E)............24 West 28th St.
Bull's Head (A)........ 322 Third Av.
Caden (E)...............166 Hudson St.
Central (E)..............253 Canal St.
Buckingham (E)....50th St. & 5th Av.
Central (E)...............272 West St.
Central Park (E)....7th Av. & 59th St.
City (E)................71 Cortlandt St.
City (A) (E)............1 Clinton Place
Clarendon (A)..........64 Union Square
Clinton Place (A)........755 Broadway
Coleman (E)..........B'way & 27th St.
Columbian (E).........187 Chatham St.
Compton (E)..............321 Third Av.
Continental (E).......B'way & 20th St.
Cooper (E)..............80 East 9th St.
Cooper Union (E).........19 Third Av.
Cosmopolitan (E) Chambers & W. B'way.
Crittenden (E)........B'way & 26th St.
Crook's (E).............84 Chatham St.
Dey Street (E)..............58 Dey St.
Earle's (A)..........Canal & Centre Sts.
Eastern (E)............62 Whitehall St.
Empire (E)...............613 Third Av.
Everett (E)..........4th Av. & 17th St.
Everett (E)...............104 Vesey St.
Farmers' (A)..............10 Broadway
Fifth Avenue (A).....5th av. & 23d St.
Frankfort (A) Frankfort & William St.
French's (E)............1 Chatham St.
Fulton (A)...............202 Third Av.
Garvey (E)..........4th Av. & 42d St.
Germania (E)............137 Grand St.
Gilsey (E)..............B'way & 29th St.

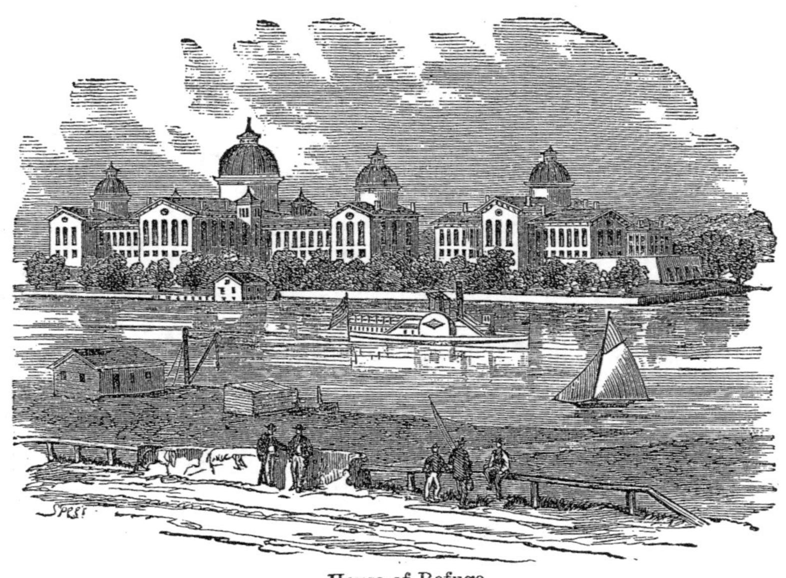

House of Refuge.

Glenham (E)..............155 Fifth Av.
Glenham (A)........3d Av. & 24th St.
Grand (E).........Broadway & 31st St.
Grand Central (A).......671 Broadway
Grand Union (E).... 4th Av. & 41st St.
Grant (E)..............48 New Bowery
Groot's (A)...............490 Canal St.
Grosvenor (A).............37 Fifth Av.
Hanfield's (E)............622 Grand St.
Hankh's (E).............435 Ninth Av.
Hartman's (E)...............47 Bowery
Hoffman (E)...............1,111 B'way
Hotel Branting (A) ....
Madison Av. & 58th St.
" Brunswick (E). ....225 5th Av.
" del Recreo (E)......11 W. 11th St.
" de Paris (E).......22 W. Houston
" de Strasbourg (A)....229 10th Av.
" de Versailles(E) 30 E. Houston St.
" Espanola (A)........21 E. 4th St.
" Germania (E).......141 Cedar St.
" Jegel (E)...........47 Barclay St.
" Menzel (E) ....29 Bowery
" St. Germain (E) (A).............
Fifth Av. & 22d St.
Hotel Vanderbilt (E) (A).............
54 & 56 Warren St.
Hygienic (A).............15 Laight St.
International (E).....17 & 19 Park Row
Irving (E).............. .49 E. 12th St.
Irving Place (A).........1 Irving place
Lafayette (E)................595 B'way
La Pierre (E)............56 Warren St.
Leggett's (E)...........46 Chatham St.
Libby (E) ....54 & 56 Warren St.
Lion Park (E)......110th St. & 8th Av.
McKinley's (E)............93 South St.
Madison Avenue (A)....63 Madison Av.
Madison Sq. (E). Broadway & 21st St.
Maltby (E) (A) 21 & 23 Great Jones St.
Manhattan (E)........... 265 Bowery,
Marlborough (A) ...6th Av. & 38th St.
Merchants (A).........39 Cortlandt St.
Metropolitan (E) (A)....586 Broadway.
Mill's (A)..................375 4th Av.
Monument (E).........6 Union Square.
National (E)............5 Cortlandt St.
New England (A)............30 Bowery
New Jersey (E)........73 Cortlandt St.
New Sailors' Home (E) (A) 338 Pearl St.
New York (A)............721 Broadway
Northern (E)......Cortlandt & West St.
Oatman (E)....................31 Bowery
Occidental (E)....Broome St. & Bowery
Old Libby (A).......... 386 Fourth Av.
Pacific (A)...........174 Greenwich St.
Pacify (E)................. 33 Bowery,
Paige's (E)..........Spring & West Sts.
Parker (E)............B'way & 34th St.
Park (E).......Beekman & Nassau Sts.
Pearl Street (E)...........309 Pearl St.
Prescott (A) (E) Broadway & Spring St.
Putnam (E)................367 4th Av.

Reinhardt's (E).........2 Greenwich St.
Remsen (A) (E)........2,398 Third Av.
Reservoir Park (E)....40th St. & 6th Av.
Revere (E)...............606 Broadway
Robinson (E)...........18 East 16th St.
Sailors' Home (A)........190 Cherry St.
Saint Charles (E).............648 B'way
" Cloud (E)........B'way & 42d St.
" Denis (E)........B'way & 11th St.
" Julien (E)....4 Washington place
" Nicholas (A)......515 Broadway.
" James (E).......26th St. & B'way
" Omer (E).......6th Av. & 23d St.
" Germain (E)
22d St. Broadway & 5th Av.
" Lawrence (E)..........31 Bowery
Sauer's Fourth Av. 26th St. & 4th Av.
Sheridan (E).............159 Canal St.
Sinclair (A) (E)............754 Broadway
Smith & McNeill's (E)
197 Washington St.
Smith's (E)............56 Chatham St.
Soule's European (E) ....
6th Av. & 44th St.
Southern (E)................679 B'way
Spingler (A)...........5 Union Square
Stacy (E)......................760 B'way
Steel's (E)...........316 Greenwich St.
Steuben (E)...................295 Bowery
Stevens (E)...................23 Broadway
Sturtevant (A).........1,186 Broadway
Summit (E)...........Canal & Bowery
Sweeney's (E) ......Duane & Chatham
Tremont (E)............ 663 Broadway
Tyler (E)......... Broadway & 12th St.
Union Place (E)......B'way & 14th St.
Union Square (E)....16 Union Square.
United States (E) .....Fulton & Water
Van Dyke (A) .... 28 Bowery
Van Dyke (E)........21 Catharine slip.
Vanderbilt (E)......... 149 Hudson St.
Warren (E)..........Canal & Elizabeth
Washington (A)............1 Broadway.
Washington (E).............375 4th Av.
Westminster (E) Irving Pl. & 16th St.
Westmoreland (E). Fourth Av. & 17th
West Side (E)...........227 Sixth Av.
Winchester (E).........B'way & 31st St.
Windsor (A)........ 5th Av. & 46th St.
Zahn's (E)..............7 East Broadway

CLUBS.

American Jockey, Madison av. cor. E. 27th.
Arion, 21 St. Mark's pl.
Army and Navy, 16 Fifth av.
Aschenbroedel, 74 E. 4th.
Blossom, 129 Fifth av.
Century, 109 E. 15th.
German Lese Verein, E. 55th, cor. Third av.
German, 104 Fourth av.

Gotham, B'way, cor. E. 14th.
Harmonie, W. 42d, near Fifth av.
Knickerbocker, Fifth av., c. E. 28th.
Lotus Club, 2 Irving pl.
Manhattan, 96 Fifth av.
New York, 309 Fifth av.
N. Y. Chess, University building.
N. Y. Caledonian, 118 Sullivan.
N. Y. Yacht Club, house at Staten Island. Madison av., c. E. 22d.
Palette, 6 E. 23d st. Madison Sq.
Sorosis.
Travelers', 124 Fifth av.
Union, W. 21st. st., c. Fifth av.
Union League, Madison av., cor. E. 26th.
Verein Freundschaft, 141 W. 31st.

BANKS.

*Those marked * are State Banks, all others are National Banks.*

AMERICAN NATIONAL.......944 B'way
AMERICAN EX. NATIONAL...126 B'way
ATLANTIC NATIONAL........17 Nassau
* BANK OF AMERICA...........46 Wall
BANK OF BRITISH NORTH AMERICA, 52 Wall
BANK OF CALIFORNIA..........33 Pine
BANK OF MONTREAL, Bell & Smithers, Agents..................59 Wall
* BANK OF N. AMERICA........44 Wall
BANK OF NEW YORK, National Banking Association.......48 Wall
* BANK OF THE METROPOLIS, 31 Union Square
BOWERY NATIONAL..........62 Bowery
* BULL'S HEAD......314 Third Avenue
CANADIAN BANK OF COMMERCE, 50 Wall
CENTRAL NATIONAL.........320 B'way
CHATHAM NATIONAL.........196 B'way
CHEMICAL NATIONAL........270 B'way
CLEARING HOUSE..............48 Wall
CONTINENTAL NATIONAL.....7 Nassau
CORBIN BANKING COMPANY, 61 Broadway
* CORN EXCHANGE..........13 William
* DRY GOODS...........347 Broadway
E. R. NATIONAL.........680 Broadway
* ELEVENTH WARD......143 Avenue D
FIFTH NATIONAL......338 Third Ave.
FIRST NATIONAL.........94 Broadway
FOURTH NATIONAL..........16 Nassau
FULTON NATIONAL..........33 Fulton
GALLATIN NATIONAL.......... 36 Wall
GERMAN-AMERICAN.........120 B'way
GERMANIA.................185 Bowery
GERMAN EXCHANGE.......245 Bowery
* GOLD EX. BANK.........58 Broadway
* GRENWICH.............402 Hudson
* GROCERS NATIONAL......59 Barclay
HANOVER NATIONAL........33 Nassau
HARLEM...........2,279 Third Avenue
IMPORTERS' AND TRADERS' NATIONAL, 247 Broadway
IRVING NATIONAL......285 Greenwich
LEATHER MANUFACTURERS' NATIONAL 29 Wall
* LOANERS'.................22 Nassau
* MANHATTAN COMPANY.......40 Wall
* MANUFACTURERS AND MERCHANTS 561 Broadway
* MANUFACTURERS & BUILDERS' ....3d Av. & 57th street
MARINE NATIONAL............78 Wall
MERKET NATIONAL...........286 Pearl
MECHANICS NATIONAL........33 Wall
MECHANICS & TRADERS' NATIONAL...............153 Bowery
MERCANTILE NATIONAL.....191 B'way
MERCHANTS' NATIONAL........42 Wall
MERCHANTS' EXCHANGE NATIONAL 257 B'way
METROPOLITAN NATIONAL...110 B'way
MURRAY HILL....3d Av. & 37th street
MUTUAL.........................Closed
NASSAU..................135 Nassau
NATIONAL BANK OF COMMERCE 29 Nassau
NATIONAL BANK OF THE STATE OF NEW YORK.............35 William
NATIONAL BANK OF THE REPUBLIC 90 Broadway
NATIONAL BANK OF THE COMMONWEALTH................15 Nassau
NATIONAL BROADWAY.......237 B'way
NATIONAL BUTCHERS & DROVERS' 124 Bowery
NATIONAL CITIZENS'........381 B'way
NATIONAL CITY...............52 Wall
NATIONAL CURRENCY........92 B'way
NATIONAL MECHANICS' BANKING ASSOCIATION.............38 Wall
NATIONAL PARK......214 & 216 B'way
NATIONAL SHOE & LEATHER, 271 B'way
N. Y. GOLD EXCHANGE.......58 B'way
" COUNTY NATIONAL...81 8th Ave.
" NATIONAL EXCHANGE, 137 Chambers
NINTH NATIONAL...........409 B'way
* NINTH WARD........23 Abingdon Sq
* NORTH RIVER.........187 Greenwich
* ORIENTAL................122 Bowery
* PACIFIC.....................47 B'way
* PEOPLE'S..................395 Canal
PHŒNIX NATIONAL.............45 Wall
* PRODUCE..............59 Park Place
SECOND NATIONAL......190 Fifth Ave
SECURITY...................319 B'way
SEVENTH WARD NATIONAL...234 Pearl
SIXTH NATIONAL......B'way & W. 35th
ST. NICHOLAS NATIONAL........7 Wall
TENTH NATIONAL...........348 B'way
THIRD NATIONAL..............29 Pine
TRADESMEN'S NATIONAL ...291 B'way

UNION NATIONAL..............34 Wall
* WEST SIDE.......8th Av., cor 34th S.

SAVINGS BANKS.

ABINGDON SQUARE....23 Abingdon sq.
BANK OF SAVINGS..........67 Bleecker
BOND ST. SAVINGS BANK.....56 Bond
BOWERY..................130 Bowery
BROADWAY... ....4 Park Place
CENTRAL PARK..........124 Third av.
CITIZENS...................58 Bowery
CLAIRMONT ....247 Greenwich
CLINTON.................244 Eighth av.
DRY DOCK...........Bowery & Third st.
EAST RIVER...............3 Chambers
EAST SIDE.................187 Cherry
EMIGRANT INDUSTRIAL...51 Chambers
ELEVENTH WARD. Av. C & Seventh st.
EQUITABLE..............170 Sixth av.
EXCELSIOR..............374 Sixth av.
FRANKLIN... ....594 Eighth av.
FIFTH AVENUE..... 44th st. & Fifth av.
GERMAN...................4 Union sq.
GERMAN UP-TOWN.......801 Third av.
GERMAN..........Third av. & 158th st.
GREENWICH..............73 Sixth av.
HARLEM.................1,948 Third av.
INSTITUTION FOR THE SAVINGS OF MERCHANTS' CLERKS....20 Union place
IRVING.......................96 Warren
MANHATTAN............ 644 Broadway
MECHANICS & TRADERS'..283 Bowery
METROPOLITAN.............1 Third av.
NATIONAL..............609 Broadway
NEW AMSTERDAM........215 Broadway
NEW YORK.............81 Eighth av.
NORTH RIVER........... 450 Eighth av.
ORIENTAL....................430 Grand
PEOPLE'S.................801 Third av.
SEAMEN'S......................76 Wall
SECURITY......... Third av. & 34th st.
SIXPENNY......Broadway, cor. 8th st.
TEUTONIA.....................25 Av. A
TRADES......................275 W. 23d
UNION DIME.................396 Canal
UP-TOWN.................811 Third av.
WEST SIDE..............154 Sixth av.
YORKVILLE.........Third av. & 86t st.

TRUST COMPANIES.

AM. LOAN AND TRUST CO....141 B'way
BANKERS & BROKERS' ASSOCIATION, 18 Broad st.
EQUITABLE TRUST CO......52 William
FARMERS' LOAN AND TRUST CO., 26 Exchange Place
MERCANTILE.... ....120 Broadway
NATIONAL TRUST CO. ....263 B'way
N. Y. GUARANTY & INDEMNITY CO., 52 B'way
N. Y. BOND DEPOSIT CO....108 B'way
N. Y. LIFE INS. & TRUST CO..52 Wall
N. Y. LOAN & INDEMNITY CO., 229 B'way
N. Y. STATE LOAN & TRUST CO., 50 Wall
REAL ESTATE LOAN AND TRUST CO. 17 B'way
UNION TRUST CO............71 B'way
UNITED STATES TRUST CO......49 Wall
U. S. MORTGAGE CO..........50 Wall

SAFE DEPOSIT CO'S.

CENTRAL SAFE DEPOSIT COMPANY OF NEW YORK......71 & 73 W. 23d st.
MERCANTILE LOAN AND WAREHOUSE COMPANY......120 to 124 Broadway
SAFE DEPOSIT CO. OF NEW YORK 140, 142, 146 B'way, cor. Liberty
N. Y. STOCK EXCHANGE ..10 Broad st.
NATIONAL PARK BANK, 214, 216 B'way
STUYVESANT SAFE DEPOSIT COMPANY, 1 and 3 Third av.

POLICE STATIONS.

Headquarters, 300 Mulberry st.
House for Detention of Witnesses, 203 Mulberry st.

Precinct.	*Location.*
1	52 New st.
4	9 Oak st.
5	19 & 21 Leonard st.
6	9 Franklin st.
7	247 Madison st.
8	128 Prince st.
9	94 Charles st.
10	89 Eldridge st.
11	Union Market
12	126 st. near Fourth av.
13	178 Delancey st.
14	205 Mulberry st.
15	221 Mercer st.
16	156 W. 20th st.
17	First av. cor. 5th st.
18	163 E. 22d st.
19	220 E. 59th st.
20	434 W. 37th st.
21	120 E. 35th st.
22	347 W. 47th st.
23	87th st. near Av. A
24	Harbor Police Boat No. 1
25	34 E. 29th st.
26	City Hall
27	Church & Liberty sts.
29	137 & 139 W. 30th st.
30	131st st. & B'way
31	100th st. bet. Ninth & Tenth avs.
32	Tenth av. & W. 152d st.
33	Morrisania
34	Tremont
35	35 King's Bridge

Sub Stations:—Grand Central Depot.
Sanitary & Detective Squads:—300 Mulberry st.

SEAMAN'S BANK FOR SAVINGS.

74 and 76 Wall Street, corner of Pearl.

DISTANCES IN THE CITY.

From Battery.	*From Custom h.*	*From City Hall.*	TO
Mile.	Mile.	Mile.	
¼	......	......	Rector st.
½	¼	......	Fulton.
¾	½	......	City Hall.
1	¾	¼	Leonard.
1¼	1	½	Canal.
1½	1¼	¾	Spring.
1¾	1½	1	E. Houston.
2	1¾	1¼	E. 4th.
2¼	2	1½	E. 9th.
2½	2¼	1¾	E. 14th.
2¾	2½	2	E. 19th.
3	2¾	2¼	E. 24th.
3¼	3	2½	E. 29th.
3½	3¼	2¾	E. 34th.
3¾	3½	3	E. 38th.
4	3¾	3¼	E. 44th.
4¼	4	3½	E. 49th.
4½	4¼	3¾	E. 54th.
4¾	4½	4	E. 58th.
5	4¾	4¼	E. 63d.
5¼	5	4½	E. 68th.
5½	5¼	4¾	E. 73d.
5¾	5½	5	E. 78th.
6	5¾	5¼	E. 83d.
6¼	6	5½	E. 88th.
6½	6¼	5¾	E. 93d.
6¾	6½	6	E. 97th.
7	6¾	6¼	E. 102d.
7¼	7	6½	E. 107th.
7½	7¼	6¾	E. 112th.
7¾	7½	7	E. 117th.
8	7¾	7¼	E. 121st.
8¼	8	7½	E. 126th.

COURTS.

POLICE COURTS.

1. District (Lower Police Office) at the Tombs, Centre, cor. of Franklin st. and City Hall.
2. District at Jefferson Market, W. 10th st., cor. of Greenwich av.
3. District at 69 Essex st.
4. District at E. 57th st., near Lexington av.
5. District at 125th st., bet. 4th and Lexington av.
6. District at Tremont.

CRIMINAL COURTS FOR THE CITY AND COUNTY OF NEW YORK.

Oyer and Terminer, New Court House.—Terms, first Monday in January, April, October and December.

General Sessions, Brown Stone Building in City Hall Park, held by the Recorder or City Judge.—Terms, first Monday in each month.

Special Sessions, Halls of Justice [Tombs], held by three Police Justices on Tuesday, Thursday and Saturday, at 9 A.M.

MARKETS.

Washington—North River, Vesey and Fulton st.

Fulton—East River, Fulton and Beekman st.

Catharine—East River and Catharine st.

Centre—Grand and Centre sts.

Essex—Grand and Ludlow sts.

Tompkins—Third avenue, 6th to 7th sts.

Jefferson—Sixth and Greenwich avs.

Clinton—North River, Canal and Spring sts.

Franklin—East River at Old Slip.

Union—Second and Houston sts.

Gouverneur Market—East River, cor. of Water and Gouverneur.

STAGE ROUTES.

BROADWAY AND FIFTH AVENUE LINE.

Leaves Fulton Ferry, and runs through

Fulton St., to	Fifth Avenue, to
Broadway, to	Forty-seventh St.
Fourteenth St., to	Ret'ns same route.

Fare, 10 cents.

From 47th St., first stage, 6.30 a.m.

From 47th St., last stage, 11.00 p.m.

From Fulton Ferry, first stage, 7.15 a.m.

From Fulton Ferry, last stage, 12.00 p.m.

BROADWAY, 23D STREET AND NINTH AVENUE LINE.

Leaves South Ferry, and runs through

Broadway, to	Ninth Avenue, to
Twenty-third St., to	Thirtieth Street.

Returns by same route. Fare, 10 cents.

From 30th St., first stage, 6.15 a.m.

From 30th St., last stage, 10.45 p.m.

From South Ferry, first stage, 6.40 a.m.

From South Ferry, last stage, 11.30 p.m.

MADISON AVENUE LINE.

Leaves Wall St. Ferry & runs through

Wall Street, to	Madison Ave., to
Broadway, to	Forty-second St.
Twenty-third St., to	Ret'n same route.

Fare, 10 cents.

From 42d St., first stage, 7.00 a.m.

From 42d St., last stage, 10.00 p.m.

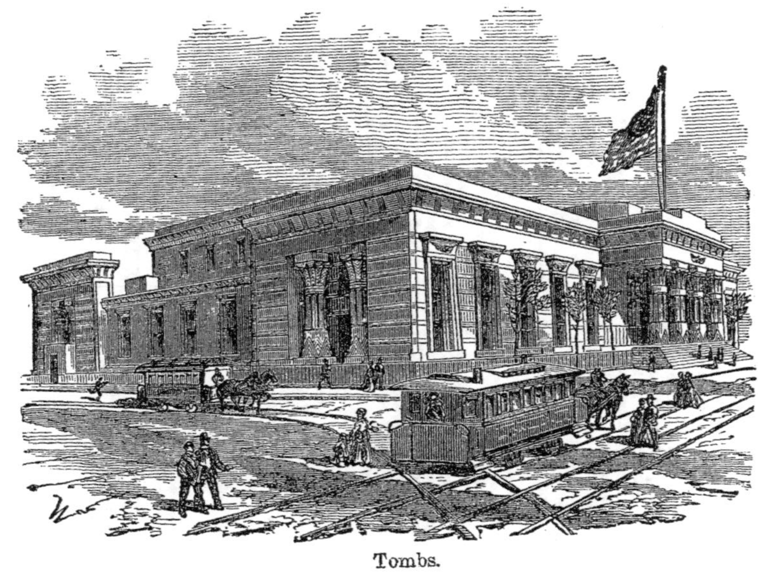

Tombs.

From Wall St. Ferry, first stage, 7.40 a.m.

From Wall St. Ferry, last stage, 10.45 p.m.

MANHATTANVILLE AND BOULEVARD LINE.

Runs to *Lion Brewery, Manhattanville, Manhattan, High Bridge, Carmansville.*

Leaves corner 32d street and Sixth avenue every 20 minutes, from 7.30 a.m. to 11.15 p.m. Runs up Broadway and Boulevard to 129th street (fare 10 cents), there transfer to stages running from 7.30 a.m. to 9.30 p.m. (fare 8 cents), to 167th street. Through fare 15 cents.

CARRIAGES AND HACK FARES.

Persons employing coaches will consult their own interests by making a bargain with the driver before entering the vehicle. Each carriage is required to have its license number conspicuously painted on its lamps, and the legal rates of fare printed and posted up within it in plain sight; and no hackman whose carriage is not so furnished can collect any fare from his customer.

Every licensed owner or driver of any hackney coach, carriage, or cab, when with his coach, carriage, or cab on any public stand, or at any of the steamboat landings or railroad depots, shall wear conspicuously on his left breast a badge in the form of a shield, of a size sufficient to admit the number of the coach to be engraved thereon in plain black figures, with the word "Licensed" above and the word "Hack" beneath such number, in semi-circular form.

Every driver of any carriage or cab shall present to every passenger employing him a card, on which shall be legibly printed the number of his license, and also the name and stable of the owner, and the number of the carriage or cab driven by him, together with the place of the Mayor's office.

In case of any violation of the law, or overcharge, passengers will report the number of the carriage at the Mayor's office (City Hall) for advice or redress.

RATES OF FARE.

1. For conveying a passenger any distance not exceeding one mile, $1.00; for two passengers the same distance, $1.50; and for every additional passenger, 50 cents.

2. For any distance exceeding a mile, and within two miles, 75 cts.; for every additional passenger, 37½ cts.

3. For the use of a carriage by the hour, with one or more passengers, with the privilege of going from place to place, and stopping as often as may be required, $1 an hour.

4. In all cases where the hiring of a hackney coach or carriage is not at the time thereof specified to be by the day or hour, it shall be deemed to be by the mile.

5. For children between 2 and 14 years of age, half price; and for children under 2 years, no charge is to be made.

6. Whenever a hackney coach or carriage shall be detained, excepting as aforesaid, the owner or driver shall be allowed after the rate of 75 cts. an hour.

In case of disagreement as to distance or price, the same shall be determined by the First Marshal.

CITY RAILROADS.

Avenue Lines.

Horse-cars run over these routes at short intervals, day and evening, and on the Third and Eighth avenues at longer intervals through the night. Fare, usually five cents per passenger.

Passengers before entering a car should inquire its route of the conductor, unless they have assured themselves by reading the inscriptions on its sides, as the cars of several routes frequently pass over portions of the same track. Many of the cars from above Canal street stop on Broadway, at the corner of Canal or Broome street, about a mile above the Astor House, the general terminus of many of the routes.

BROADWAY AND UNIVERSITY PLACE LINE — Leaves corner Broadway and Barclay st. Runs through Barclay st. to Church, to Canal, to Greene, to Clinton pl., to University pl., to Union sq., to Broadway, to Seventh av., to Fifty-ninth st., to Central Park. Returns by same route to University pl., to Wooster st., crosses Canal st. to West Broadway, to College pl., to Barclay st. to starting point. Last car leaves Central Park at 1 a.m.; last car leaves Barclay st., at 1.45 a.m. Office, Seventh av. cor. W. 51st st.

BROADWAY AND BROOME STREET LINE. — Leaves corner Broadway and Broome st. Runs through Broome st. to Greene st., and thence by same route as Broadway and University pl. line.

Returns by same route as Broadway and University pl. to Broome st., thence to Broadway. Last car leaves Central Park 10.30 p.m.; last car leaves Broome st. 11.05 p.m. Office, Seventh av. cor. W. 51st st.

SIXTH AVENUE LINE.—Leaves corner Broadway and Vesey st. Runs through Vesey st. to Church st., to Chambers st., to West Broadway, to Canal st., to Varick st., to Carmine st., to Sixth av., to Fifty-ninth st. and Central Park. Returns by the same route to West Broadway, to College pl., to Vesey st., to cor. Broadway. Runs all night. Office, 756 Sixth av.

SIXTH AVENUE, BROADWAY AND CANAL ST. LINE.—Leaves corner Broadway and Canal st. Runs through Canal st. to Varick st., thence by same route as Sixth av. line. Returns by same route. Last car leaves Forty-third st. depot at 11.20 p.m.; last car leaves Broadway and Canal st. at 10.54 p.m. Office, 756 Sixth av.

SEVENTH AVENUE LINE.—Leaves Broadway and Park Pl. Runs through Park pl. to Church, to Canal, to Sullivan, to W. 4th, to Macdougal, to Clinton pl., to Greenwich av., to Seventh av., to Fifty-ninth st. and Central Park. Returns by same route, to Greenwich av., to Clinton pl., to Macdougal, to W. 4th, to Thompson, to Canal, to W. Broadway, to Park pl., to Broadway. Last car leaves Central Park at 11 p.m.; last car leaves Broadway at 11.46. p.m. Office, Seventh av., cor. W. 51st st.

EIGHTH AVENUE LINE.—Leaves Broadway and Vesey st. Runs through Vesey st. to Church, to Chambers, to W. Broadway, to Canal st., to Hudson, to Eighth av., to Fifty-ninth st., and Central Park and 141st st. Returns by same route. This line runs every 15 minutes all night. Office, Eighth av. cor. W. 50th st.

EIGHTH AVENUE, BROADWAY AND CANAL ST. LINE.—Leaves Broadway and Canal st., to Hudson st., thence up and down same route as Eighth av. line, returning to Canal st. and Broadway. Last car leaves Broadway and Canal st. at 10.55 p.m.; last car leaves 49th st. depot at 10.20 p.m. Office, Eighth av. cor. W. 50th st.

NEW YORK ELEVATED RAILWAY.—From Morris st. and Greenwich, via Greenwich to W. 12th st.; then via 9th av. to 59th st. Stations at Morris, Dey, Canal, W. 12th and W. 29th sts. Trains connect with Hudson R. R. R. Office, 7 Broadway.

NINTH AVENUE LINE.—Leaves Broadway and Fulton street. Runs through Fulton st. to Greenwich to 9th av., to Fifty-fourth st. Returns by same route to Washington st., to Fulton, to Broadway. Last car leaves Broadway, cor. Fulton, at 9.45 p.m.; last car leaves 54th st. depot at 9 p.m. Office, 816 Ninth av.

CENTRAL PARK, NORTH AND EAST RIVER LINE.—Leaves South Ferry. Runs through Whitehall st. to Marketfield, to Bowling Green, to Battery pl., to West st., to Tenth av., to Fifty-ninth st., to Central Park. Returns by same route. Last car leaves cor. Fifty-ninth st. and Tenth av., 10.30 p.m.; South Ferry, 11.30 p.m. Office, Tenth av., cor. W. 54th.

SECOND AVENUE LINE.—Leaves foot of Peck slip. Runs through South st. to Oliver, to Bowery, to Grand st., to Chrystie, to Houston, to Second av., to 128th st., Harlem. Returns by Second av., to Twenty-third st., to First av., to Houston st., to Allen, to Grand, to Bowery, to Chatham st., to Pearl, to starting point, also from ft. E. 92d, to Av. A, to E. 86th, to Second av., to Stuyvesant st., to Astor pl., to Broadway, returning same route. Cars run from Peck slip all night. Cars run from Sixty-third st. all night; last car leaves Harlem at 1 a.m.; last car leaves Sixty-third st. for Harlem at 12.30 a.m. This line also runs to B'way and Worth st. Offices, 34 New st. and Second av., cor. E. 63d.

THIRD AVENUE LINE.—Leaves Broadway, opposite Astor House. Runs through Park row to Chatham st., to Bowery, to Third av., to Sixty-fifth st., thence to Harlem. Returns by same route. Cars on this line run all night. For Grand Central Depot. Leaves Broadway, opposite Astor House. Runs through Park row, to Chatham st., to Bowery, to Third av., to Thirty-fifth st., to Lexington av., to Railroad Depot. Returns by same route. Last car from Depot 11 p.m. This line also runs to Broadway and Worth st. Offices, cor. E. 34th st., E. 65th st., and 2,390 Third av.

FOURTH AVENUE LINE.—Leaves Broadway, opposite the Astor House. Runs through Park row to Centre st., to Grand, to Bowery, to Fourth av., to Forty-second st., from 42d st. to Grand Central Depot, Madison av., to E. 86th. Every third car continues through Thirty-second st. to Lexington av., to Thirty-fourth st., to Hunter's Point Ferry. Returns by same route to Broome st., to Centre, to starting point. Last car leaves Astor House at 12 p.m.: last car leaves Thirty-fourth st. Ferry at 10.45 p.m.: last car leaves Thirty-second st. Depot at 11 p.m.

MADISON AV. LINE.—From Broadway opposite Astor House. Runs through Park row to Centre, to Grand, to Bowery, to Fourth av., to Forty-second st., to Madison av., to Eighty-sixth st. Returns by same route to Broome, to Centre, to starting point. Last car from Eighty-sixth st. at 9 p.m., also at 12 p.m. to depot at Thirty-second st. Last car from Astor House at 10 p.m.

CITY HALL, AVENUE B AND THIRTY-FOURTH STREET LINE.—Leaves Ann street and Broadway. Runs through Park row to Chatham st., to East Broadway, to Clinton st., to Avenue B, to Fourteenth st., to Avenue A, to Twenty-third st., to First av., to Thirty-fourth st., to Ferry. Returns by same route to Second st., to Avenue A, to Essex st., to East Broadway, to Chatham st., to Park row, to Ann st. and Broadway. Last car leaves Thirty-fourth st. at 11.46 p.m.; last car leaves Broadway and Ann st. at 12.30 a.m.

FORTY-SECOND AND GRAND ST. FERRY LINE.—From ft. W. 42d to Tenth av., to W. 34th, to Broadway, to E. 23d, to Fourth av., to E. 14th, to Avenue A, to E. Houston, to Cannon, to Grand, to Ferry; returning through Grand to Goerck, to E. Houston, to Second, to Av. A, to E. 14th, to Fourth av., to E. 23d, to Broadway, to W. 34th, to Tenth av., to ft. W. 42d.

DRY DOCK AND EAST BROADWAY LINE.—Leaves Ann st. and Broadway. Runs through Park row to Chatham st., to East Broadway, to Grand st., to Columbia, to Avenue D, to Tenth st., to Avenue A, to E. 23d. Returns by Tenth st. to Avenue D, to Eighth st., to Lewis, to Grand, thence by same route to starting point. Last car leaves 14th st. and Avenue A at 11 p.m.; last car leaves Broadway and Ann st. at 11.33 p.m.

THIRTY-FOURTH STREET BRANCH.—From E. 34th to Depot, Avenue B, to Second, to Essex, to East Broadway, to Chatham, to Ann. Returning to Chatham, to East Broadway, to Clinton, to Avenue B, to E. 14th, to Avenue A, to E. 23d, to First av., to 34th st. Ferry. Offices, 605 Grand and E. 14th cor. Avenue B.

CENTRAL PARK, EAST RIVER AND AVENUE A LINE. — Leaves South Ferry, foot of Whitehall st. Runs through Whitehall st. to Front, to Old Slip, to South st., to Grand, to Goerck, to Houston, to Avenue D, to Fourteenth st., to Avenue A, to Twenty-third st., to First av., to Fifty-ninth st., to Fifth av. to Central Park. Returns by Fifty-ninth st., takes same route to Avenue D, and Seventh st., to Lewis, to Houston, to Mangin, to Grand, to Corlears, to Monroe, to Jackson, to Front, to Water, to South Ferry. This road passes all the East River Ferries. Last car leaves South Ferry at 11 p.m.; last car leaves 59th st. and 5th av. at 9.45 p.m.

CROSS TOWN LINES.

GRAND AND CORTLANDT ST. LINE.—Leaves Grand st. Ferry. Runs through Grand to East B'way, to Canal, to Walker, to West B'way, North Moore, Washington to Cortlandt st. Ferry. Returns by Cortlandt, Greenwich, Beach, West B'way, Lispenard, to Broadway, to Canal, and then by same route to starting point. Last car from Grand st. Ferry at 11 p.m. Last car from Cortlandt st. Ferry at 11.35 p.m.

BLEECKER ST. AND FULTON FERRY LINE. — Leaves Fulton Ferry. Runs through Fulton st. to William, to Ann, to Park row, to Centre st., to Leonard, to Elm, to Howard, to Crosby, to Bleecker, to Macdougal, to Fourth, to W. Twelfth, to Hudson, to Fourteenth, to Eleventh av., to foot W. 23d st. Returns by Tenth av., to Fourteenth st., to Hudson, to Bleecker, to Crosby, to Howard, to Elm, to Reade, to Centre, to Beekman, to South, to Fulton Ferry. Last car leaves Fulton Ferry at 12.50 a.m.; last car leaves Fourteenth st., and Tenth av., at 12 p.m. Office, 18 Tenth av.

BLEECKER ST. BRANCH. — Leaves Fulton Ferry. Runs through Fulton st., to Water, to Peck Slip, to Pearl, to New Bowery, to Bowery, to Canal st., to Elm, to Howard, to Crosby, thence by same route as the above road. Returns by same route to Canal st., to Bowery, to New Bowery, to Pearl, to Peck Slip, to South, to Fulton Ferry. Last car leaves Fulton Ferry at 12.08 a.m.; last car leaves 14th st. and 11th av. at 11.20 p.m. Office, 18 Tenth av.

DESBROSSES, VESTRY AND GRAND ST. LINE. — Leaves Grand st. Ferry. Runs through Grand st. to Sullivan, to Vestry, to Greenwich, to Desbrosses, to Desbrosses st. Ferry. Returns by Desbrosses st. to Washington, to Vestry, thence by same route to starting point. Last car leaves Grand st. Ferry at 12 p.m.; last car leaves Desbrosses st. Ferry at 12.30 p.m. Office foot of Grand st., E. R.

CHURCH ST. TO SOUTH FERRY.—From cor. Church st. and Vesey, via New Church, Greenwich, State to South Ferry. Returning via Whitehall, Battery pl., Greenwich, New Church to Vesey st. Fare 5 cents.

HOUSTON, WEST ST. AND PAVONIA FERRY.—Leaves Erie depot, Chambers and West st. Runs through West st., to Charlton, Prince, Bowery, Stanton, Pitt, Avenue C, Eighteenth st., Avenue A, Twenty-third st., First av., Thirty-fifth st., Lexington av., Forty-second st., Gr. Cen. Depot. Returns by Forty-second st., Lexington av., Thirty-sixth st., First av., Twenty third st., Avenue A, Seventeenth st., Avenue C, Third st., First av., Houston st., West st., to Chambers st. Last car leaves Grand Central Depot at 11.15 p.m. Last car leaves Chambers st., at 12.35 p.m. Office, 415 E. 10th st.

125TH ST.—From 3d av. cor. E. 130th, through 3d av. to E. 125th, to W. 125th, returning same route.

HARLEM BRIDGE, MORRISANIA AND FORDHAM.—From Harlem Br. up 3d av. to Fordham, also from Harlem Br. up 3d av. to Boston av., up Boston av. to W. Farms. Fare 6 cents to Morrisania, 8 cents to Tremont, 10 cents to Fordham, 10 cents to W. Farms.

23D ST.—From foot of and through W. 23d to E. 23d, to E. River. Returning same route, also from foot of and through W. 23d, to E. 23d, to 2d av., to E. 28th, to 1st av., to E. 34th st. Ferry. Returning through 1st av., to E. 29th st., to 2d av., to E. 23d, and through to foot W. 23d st. Fare 5 cents.

HOBOKEN AND GREENPOINT FERRY LINE.—From Hoboken Ferry, foot Christopher, via Christopher to 8th st. Avenue A and E. 10th to Greenpoint Ferry, foot of E. 23d st. Returning via E. 10th, Avenue A, 9th, Stuyvesant, 8th, Greenwich av., West 10th, West st. to Hoboken Ferry, ft. of Christopher st.; also via Christopher, Greenwich av., W. 11th st., Seventh av., 14th st., Union Square, Broadway, E. 17th, Avenue A, to Greenpoint Ferry ft. of E. 23d st. Returning via Avenue A, E. 18th st., Broadway, 14th st., 7th av., 11th, West, to Christopher st. ferry. Fare 5 cents. Last car leaves Christopher st. at 12 p.m. Office Avenue A, cor. E. 22d st.

FERRIES.

The fare on most of the ferries to New Jersey is 3 cents for each passenger, and on Brooklyn ferries from 1 to 4 cents.

Astoria, from 92d st., E. R., from 5 a.m. to 10 p.m. Fare 4 cts.

Astoria, from Peck sl., E. R., to Astoria by Harlem boats.

Bay Ridge, L. I., foot of Wall st., 6 trips per day, Fare 15 cts.

Blackwell's Island, from 26th st., E. R., to Blackwell's Island, 10.30 a.m., 1.30 p.m., every day by steamboat.

Blackwell's Island, from 61st st., E. R., to Blackwell's Island; row-boat for attachés of Institution.

Bedloe's Island, from pier 58, N. R. U. S. Government boat stops at Pier 1, E. R. Pass.

Brooklyn, from Catharine st., E. R., to Main st., runs all night.

Brooklyn, from Fulton st., E. R., to Fulton st., all night.

Brooklyn, South Ferry, from Whitehall st., E. R., to Atlantic st., all night.

Brooklyn, from Whitehall st., E. R., to Hamilton av., runs all night.

Brooklyn, from Wall st., E. R., to Montague st. from 6 a.m. to 11 p.m.

Brooklyn, E. D., from Grand st., E. R., to Grand st.; from 5 a.m. to 10 p.m.

Brooklyn, E. D., from Houston st., E. R., to Grand st., runs all night.

Brooklyn, E. D., from Grand st., E. R., to South 7th street, runs all night.

Brooklyn, E. D., from Roosevelt st., E. R., to South 7th st., runs all night.

David's Island, Fort Schuyler and Willet's Point, from Pier 1, E. R., on Tuesday and Friday, U. S. Government boat, only, at 9 a.m.

Governor's Island, from Pier 1, E. R., runs daily at 7.30, 8 a.m., then every hour to 6 p.m.

Greenpoint, from Tenth st., E. R., from 4.45 a.m. to 1 a.m.

Greenpoint, from Twenty-third st., E. R., from 4.45 a.m. to 1 a.m.

Harlem, from Pier 22, E. R.

Harlem, from Pier 24, E. R.

Hart's Island, from Twenty-sixth st., E. R., to Hart's Island, 7 and 10.30 a.m., by steamboat, on Saturdays only.

Hoboken, from Barclay st., N. R., runs all night.

Hoboken, from Christopher st., N. R., from 5 a.m. to 12 p.m.

Hunter's Point, from James' sl., E. R., to Hunter's Point, 7 a.m. until 7 p.m.

Hunter's Point, from Thirty-fourth st. E. R., runs all night.

Jersey City, from Desbrosses st., N. R., runs all night.

Jersey City, from Cortlandt st., N. R., runs all night.

Jersey City, from Liberty st., N. R., to Central R. R. of N. J. dock, Communipaw, runs all night.

Jersey City, from Chambers st., N. R., to Pavonia Ferry, Erie R. R. dock, runs all night.

Jersey City, from Twenty-third st., N. R., to Pavonia Ferry, Erie R. R. dock, from 5.45 a.m. until 1.30 a.m.

Randall's Island, from Twentieth Street, E. R., to Randall's Island, 10.30 a.m.

Randall's Island, from 122d st., E. R., to Randall's Island, by row-boat, at all hours of the day.

Staten Island (New Brighton, Snug Harbor, West Brighton, Port Richmond, Elm Park), from foot Whitehall, from 6 a.m. to 9 p.m., every hour, and a last boat at 11.45 p.m.

Staten Island, People's North Shore Weehawken, ft. of W. 42d st., fare 12 cts.

LOCATION OF PIERS.

NORTH RIVER.

NO.	FOOT OF STREET.	NO.	FOOT OF STREET.	NO.	FOOT OF STREET.
1,	Battery place.	23	Vesey.	43	Spring.
2, 3,	Battery place and Morris	24	Vesey and Barclay.	44	Spring and Charlton.
4	Morris.	25	Barclay.	45	Charlton.
5, 6, 7	Morris and Rector.	26	Barclay and Park Place.	46	King.
8	Rector.	27	Park Place.	47	West Houston.
9, 10,	Rector and Carlisle.	28	Murray.	48	Clarkson.
11	Carlisle.	29	Warren,	49	Leroy.
12	Albany.	30	Chambers.	50	Morton.
13	Albany and Cedar.	31	Duane.	51	Christopher.
14	Cedar.	32	Duane and Jay.	52	West 10th.
15	Liberty.	33	Jay.	53	Charles.
16	Liberty and Cortlandt.	34	Harrison.	54	Perry.
17, 18,	Cortlandt.	35	Franklin.	55	West 11th.
19	Cortlandt and Dey.	36	North Moore.	56	Bethune.
20	Dey.	37	Beach.	57	Horatio.
21	Fulton.	38	Hulbert.	58	Gansevoort.
22	Fulton and Vessey.	39	Vestry.	59	Bogart.
		40	Watts.	60	Bloomfield.
		41	Hoboken.	61	Little 12th.
		42	Canal.	62	West 13th
				63	West 15th.

EAST RIVER.

NO.	FOOT OF STREET.	NO.	FOOT OF STREET.	NO.	FOOT OF STREET.
1, 2	Whitehall.	27	Dover.	50	Montgomery.
3, 4	Moore and Broad.	28	Dover and Roosevelt.	51, 52	Gouverneur.
5	Broad and Coenties slip.	29	Roosevelt.	53	Jackson.
6, 7, 8	Coenties slip.	30	Roosevelt and James slip.	54	Corlears.
9, 10,	Coenties Old slip.	31, 32	James slip.	55	Cherry.
11, 12	Old slip.	33	Oliver.	56, 57	Broome.
13	Old slip & Gouverneur lane.	34, 35	Catharine.	58, 59	Delancey.
14	Jones' lane.	36	Catharine and Market.	60	Rivington.
15, 16	Wall.	37, 38	Market.	61	Rivington and Stanton.
17	Pine.	39	Market and Pike.	62	Stanton.
18	Maiden Lane.	40, 41	Pike.	63	Third.
19	Fletcher.	42	Pike and Rutgers.	64	Fifth.
20, 21	Burling slip.	43, 44	Rutgers.	65	Sixth.
22	Fulton.	45	Rutgers and Jefferson.	66	Seventh.
23	Beekman.	46	Jefferson.	67	Eighth.
24	Beekman and Peck slip.	47	Jefferson and Clinton.	68	Ninth.
25, 26	Peck slip.	48	Clinton.	69	East 10th.
		49	Clinton and Montgomery.	70	East 11th.

GRAND CENTRAL DEPOT, Fourth Avenue and 42d Street, New York.

TRAVELERS' DIRECTORY.

IN NEW YORK CITY.

RAILROADS.

Baltimore & Ohio.—Depot, Jersey City Ferries.

☞ See Taintor's New York, Philadelphia and Washington Route Guide.

Central of New Jersey.—Depot foot of Liberty street.

☞ See Taintor's New York Central R. R. Guide.

Delaware, Lackawanna & Western.—Depot, Hoboken Ferries, Barclay and Christopher sts.

Erie Railway.—Depot, Pier 30, foot of Chambers st., and Twenty-third street Ferry.

☞ See Taintor's Erie Railway Guide.

Fall River and Boston.—Pier 28, N. R. Passengers leave by steamboats (touching at Newport) to Fall River.

☞ See Taintor's Newport Guide.

Flushing and North-Side.—Foot James slip and foot E. 34th street.

Hackensack & New York.—Foot Chambers street.

Hudson River.—W. 30th, cor. Tenth avenue.

☞ See Taintor's Hudson River Railway Guide.

Long Island R. R.—Depot, James slip.

Morris & Essex.—Foot Barclay and foot Christopher.

☞ See Taintor's Morris and Essex Railway Guide.

N. J. Southern.—Foot of Murray st. Direct Route to Long Branch.

N. J. Midland.—Depot, foot of Cortlandt st., Jersey City Ferries.

New York Central.—Grand Central Depot, Forty-second st., and Fourth Avenue.

☞ See Taintor's Route Guide Hudson River R. R., and N. Y. Central R. R.

New York & Boston.—Fourth av. and Forty-second street.

☞ See Taintor's Shore Line Route Guide.

New York & Harlem.—Fourth av. and Forty-second street.

☞ See Taintor's Harlem Railroad Route Guide.

New York & New Haven.—Fourth av. and Forty-second street.

☞ See Taintor's Shore Line Route Guide.

North Shore, Staten Island.—Pier 19, North River.

Pennsylvania Central.—Depot ft. of Cortlandt and foot of Desbrosses sts.

☞ See Taintor's New York, Philadelphia and Washington Route Guide.

South-Side of Long Island.—Pier 31, East River.

☞ See Taintor's South-Side R. R. Guide.

Staten Island.—Foot of Whitehall, Pier No. 1 East River.

COASTWISE AND RIVER STEAMBOATS FROM NEW YORK.

FROM NORTH RIVER PIERS.

CAPS *denote lines running all the year round—others only until the close of river navigation.*

Albany Day Line. Fr. Pier 39. *Daniel Drew* and *C. Vibbard.* 8.10 a.m.; 24th st., 8.30 a.m.; beginning May 24th. Miles, 145. Fare, $2.

Albany, People's Line. Fr. Pier 41. *Drew* and *Dean Richmond.* Daily. 6 p.m. Miles, 145. Fare, $2.

Athens. Fr. Pier 42. *New Champion.* Tuesday, Thursday and Saturday, 6 p.m. Miles, 120. Fare, 50 cents.

Athens. Fr. Pier 35. *Andrew Harder* and *Monitor.* Daily, 5 p.m. Miles, 120. Fare, $1.

Barrytown. Fr. Pier 35. *Ansonia* and *Monitor.* Daily, 5 p.m. Miles, 95. Fare, $1.00.

Bergen Point. Fr. Pier 14. *Chancellor.* Daily, 11 a.m. and 5 p.m. Miles, 7. Fare, 15 cents.

BOSTON AND PROVIDENCE [Neptune Line]. Fr. Pier 27. *Electra* and *Galatea.* Daily, 5 p.m. in Summer. 4 p.m. in Winter. Miles, 225. Fare, $4.

BOSTON, VIA. FALL RIVER AND NEWPORT. Fr. Pier 28. *Bristol* and *Providence.* Daily, 5 p.m. in Summer. 4 p.m. in Winter. Miles, 220. Fare, $4.

BOSTON, VIA. STONINGTON. Fr. Pier 33. *Stonington* and *Rhode Island.* Daily, 5 p.m. in Summer. 4 p.m. in Winter. Miles, 225. Fare, $4.00.

BOSTON [Nor. and Wor. Line]. Fr. Pier 40. *City of Boston* and *City of New York.* Daily. 5 p.m. in Summer. 4 p.m. in Winter. Miles, 240. Fare, $4.

Catskill. Fr. Pier 39. *Daniel Drew* and *C. Vibbard.* Daily, 8.10 a.m.; 24th st., 8.30 a.m.; beginning May 24th. Miles, 115. Fare, $1.50.

Catskill. Fr. Pier 35. *Monitor* and *Andrew Harder.* Daily, at 5 p.m. Miles, 115. Fare, 50 cents.

Catskill. Fr. Pier 49. *Thomas McManus.* Monday, Wednesday, and Friday. 6 p.m. Miles, 115. Fare, 50 cents.

Catskill. Fr. Pier 42. *New Champion.* Tuesday. Thursday, and Saturday. 6 p.m. Miles, 115. Fare, 50 cents.

Chelsea. Fr. Pier 34. *G.T. Olyphant.* Daily, 3 p.m. Miles, 18. Fare, 20 cents.

Coxsackie. Fr. Pier 49. *Redfield* and *T. McManus.* Daily, 6 p.m. Miles, 126. Fare, $1.00.

Cornwall. Fr. Pier 39. *Daniel Drew* and *C. Vibbard.* Daily, 8.10 a.m.; 24th st., 8.30 a.m.; from May 24th.

Cornwall. Fr. Pier 39. *Mary Powell.* Daily, 3.30 p.m. Miles. 56. Fare, 75c.

Cornwall. Fr. Fulton st., Brooklyn, 8 a.m.; W. 10th st., 8.30 a.m.; 24th st., 9 a.m.; Sundays only. *Long Branch.* Miles, 56. Fare, $1.00.

Cornwall. Fr. Pier 43. *J. W. Baldwin* and *Thos. Cornell.* Daily, 4 p.m. Miles, 56. Fare, 50 cents.

Cornwall. Fr. Pier 35. *A. Harder* and *Monitor.* Daily, 5 p.m. Miles, 56. Fare, 50 cents.

Cozzens. Fr. Pier 39. *Mary Powell.* Daily, 3.30 p.m. Miles, 52. Fare, 75 cents.

Dobbs' Ferry. Fr. Pier 34. *Adelphi.* Daily, 4 p.m. Miles, 22. Fare, 30 cents.

Elizabethport. Fr. Pier 14. *Chancellor.* Daily, 11 a.m. and 5 p.m. Miles, 14. Fare, 20 cents.

ELIZABETHPORT. Fr. Pier 34. *Mattewan.* Sunday only. 9 a.m. Miles, 14. Fare, 25 cents.

Elm Park. Fr. Pier 19. People's North Shore Ferry. Miles, 11. Fare, 10 cents.

Englewood. Fr. Pier 20. *Alexis.* Daily, 5 p.m. Miles, 13. Fare, 20 cents.

Englewood. Fr. Pier 20. *Adelphi.* 4 p.m. Miles, 13. Fare, 20 cents.

Esopus. Fr. Pier 43. *J. W. Baldwin* and *Thomas Cornell.* Daily, 4 p.m. Miles, 84. Fare, $1.25.

FACTORYVILLE; West Brighton. Fr. Pier 19. People's North Shore Ferry. Miles, 9. Fare, 10 cents.

Fair Haven. Fr. Pier 35. See "Red Bank."
FALL RIVER. Fr. Pier 28. *Bristol* and *Providence*. Daily, 5 p.m. in Summer. 4 p.m in Winter. Miles, 170. Fare, $3.50.
Fisher's Dock, N. J. Fr. Pier 34. *G. T. Olyphant*. Daily, 3 p.m. Miles, 37. Fare, 50 cents.
Fort Lee. Fr. Pier 42. *Pleasant Valley* and *Fort Lee*. Daily, 10 a.m.; 1 and 5.15 p.m. Stops at 24th st. Sundays, every hour, from 9 a.m to 7 p.m. Miles, 12. Fare, 15 cents.
FREEHOLD. Fr. Pier 34. *Matteawan* Daily, 4 p.m. Miles, 30. Fare, 75 cents.
Germantown. Fr. Pier 35. *A. Harder* and *Monitor*.
Grassy Point. Fr. Pier 34. *Chrystenah*. Daily, 3.30 p.m. Miles, 42. Fare, 45 cents.
Governor's Island. Propeller *Governor's Island*. From Whitehall every hour from 7.30 a.m.; then hourly from 8 a.m. to 7 p.m. Miles, — Fare, 15 cents.
Hastings. Fr. Pier 34. *Alexis*. Daily, 5 p.m. Miles, 21. Fare, 30 cents.
Haverstraw. Fr. Pier 34. *Crystenah* and *Adelphi*. Daily, 3.30 and 4 p.m. Miles, 40. Fare, 40 cents.
Highland, N. Y. Fr. Pier 35. Propel. *J. L. Hasbrouck* and *D. S. Miller*. Daily, 5 p.m. Miles, 77. Fare, $1.
HIGHLANDS, N. J. Fr. Pier 35, *Helen*. Daily. Miles, 26. Fare, 50 cents.
Highland Falls. Fr. Pier 43. *Thos. Cornell*. Tuesdays, Thursdays and Saturdays, 4 p.m. Miles, 50. Fare, 50 cents.
Highland Falls. Fr. Pier 42. *New Champion*. Tuesdays, Thursdays and Saturdays, 6 p.m. Miles, 50. Fare, 50 cents.
Hudson. Fr. Pier 39. *Daniel Drew* and *C. Vibbard*. Daily, 8.10 a.m.; W. 24th street, 8.30 a.m. Miles, 120. Fare, $1.50.
Hudson. Fr. Pier 49. *Thos. McManus* and *Redfield*. Daily, 6 p.m. Miles, 120. Fare, $1.
Hyde Park. Fr. Pier 35. *Andrew Harder* and *Monitor*. Daily, 5 p.m. Miles, 81. Fare $1.
Iona Island. Fr. Fulton st., Brooklyn, 8 a.m.; W. 10th st., 8.30 a.m.; 24th st., 9 a.m. Sundays only *Long Branch*. Miles, 47. Fare, $1.
KEYPORT. Fr. Pier 34. *Matteawan*. Daily, 4 p.m. Sundays also (50 cents), 9 a.m. and 7 p.m. Miles, 27. Fare, 30 cents.
Kingston. See "Rondout."
Linoleumville. Fr. Pier 34. *G. T. Olyphant*. Daily, 3 p.m. Miles, 19. Fare, 25 cents.
Little Washington. Fr. Pier 34. *G. T. Olyphant* (connects by stage). Daily, 3 p.m. Miles, 40. Fare, 50 cents.
Locust Point. Fr. Pier 35. *Helen*. For time of leaving New York, see "Red Bank." Miles, 30. Fare, 50 cents.
LONG BRANCH. Fr. Pier 8, N. J. Southern R. R. Line. Miles, 34. Fare, $1.
Malden. Fr. Pier 35. *Andrew Harder* and *Monitor*. Daily, 5 p.m. Miles, 105. Fare, $1.
Malden. Fr. Pier 42. *New Champion*. Tuesdays, Thursdays and Saturdays, 6 p.m. Miles, 105. Fare, 50 cents.
MARINER'S HARBOR. Fr. Pier 14. Daily, 11 a.m., 5 p. m. Miles, 11. Fare, 15 cents.
Marlborough. Fr. Pier 39. *Mary Powell*. Daily, 3.30 p.m. Miles, 68. Fare, $1.
Marlborough. Fr. Pier 35. Propel. *J. L. Hasbrouck* and *D. S. Miller*. Daily, 5 p.m. Miles, 68. Fare 75 cents.
Marlborough. Fr. Pier 43. *J. W. Baldwin* and *Thos. Cornell*. Daily, 4 p.m. Miles, 68. Fare, $1.
Matawan, N. J. Fr. Pier 34. *Matteawan* (stage from Keyport). Daily, 4 p.m. Miles, 28. Fare, 40 cents.
Milton. Fr. Pier 39. *Mary Powell*. Daily, 3.30 p.m. Miles, 72. Fare, $1.
Milton. Fr. Pier 43. *J. W. Baldwin* and *Thos. Cornell*. Daily, 4 p.m. Miles, 72. Fare, $1.
Newark. Fr. Pier 22. *Thos. P. Way*. Sundays only. 10.30 a.m. Miles, 20. Fare 25 cents.
New Brighton. Fr. Pier 19. People's North Shore Ferry. Miles, 7. Fare, 10c.
Newburg. Fr. Pier 39. *Daniel Drew* and *C. Vibbard*. Daily, 8.10 a.m. W. 24th st., 8.30 a.m. Miles, 60. Fare, 75 cents.

Newburg. Fr. Pier 39. *Mary Powell.* Daily, 3.30 p.m. Miles, 60. Fare, 75c.
Newburg. Fr. Pier 43. *J. W. Baldwin* and *Thos. Cornell.* Daily, 4 p.m. Miles, 60. Fare, 50 cents.
Newburg. Fr. Pier 35. Homer, Ramsdell & Co.'s Line of Barges. Daily, 5 p.m. Miles, 60. Fare, 75 cents.
Newburg. Fulton st., Brooklyn, 8 a.m.; W. 10th st., 8.30 a.m.; W. 24th st., 9 a.m. Long Branch, Sundays only. Miles, 60. Fare, 75 cents.
New Hamburg. Fr. Pier 39. *Mary Powell.* Daily, 3.30 p.m. Miles 67. Fare, $1.
New Hamburg. Fr. Pier 35. Propel. *J. L. Hasbrouck* and *D. S. Miller.* Daily, 5 p.m. Miles, 67. Fare, 75 cents.
NEW HAVEN. Fr. Pier 18. *J. B. Schuyler.* Daily, 4 p.m. Miles, 76. Fare, $1.25.
NEW HAVEN Sundays only. Vesey st., 8 a.m.; Fulton st., Brooklyn, 8.15; Grand st., New York, 8.30; E. 23d st., 8.45 a.m. *Magenta.* Miles, 76. Fare, $1.
NEW LONDON. Fr. Pier 40. *City of New York* and *City of Boston.* Daily, 5 p.m. Miles, 120. Fare, $2,25.
NEWPORT. Fr. Pier 28. *Bristol* and *Providence.* Daily, 5 p.m. Miles 155. Fare, $3.50.
NORWICH. Fr. Pier 40. *City of Norwich.* Tuesday, Thursday and Saturday, 5 p.m. Miles, 133. Fare, $2.50.
Nyack. Fr. Pier 39. *Daniel Drew* and *C. Vibbard* (by ferry). Daily, 8.10 a.m.; W. 24th st., 8.30 a.m. Miles, 28. Fare, 40 cents.
Nyack. Fr. Pier 34. *Chrystenah.* Daily, 3.30 p.m. (Stops at W. 24th st.) Miles, 28. Fare, 35 cents.
Nyack. Fr. Pier 34. *Adelphi.* Daily, 4 p.m. Miles, 28. Fare, 35 cents.
Nyack. Fr. Pier 34. *Alexis.* Daily, 5 p.m. Miles, 28. Fare 35 cents.
Oceanic, N. J. Fr. Pier 35. *Helen.* Daily, according to tide. Miles, 28. Fare, 50 cents.
Peekskill. Fr. Pier 34. *Chrystenah.* Daily, 3.30 p.m. (Stops at W. 24th st.) Miles, 48. Fare, 45 cents.
PERTH AMBOY. Fr. Pier 34. *G. T. Olyphant.* Daily, 3 p.m. Miles, 24. Fare, 25 cents.
PERTH AMBOY. From Pier 34. *Matteawan.* Sundays only, 9 a m. Miles, 24. Fare, 25 cents.
Pleasant Valley. Fr. Pier 42. *Pleasant Valley* and *Fort Lee.* Daily, 10 a.m., 2, 5.15 p.m. (stops at 24th st.); Sundays, every hour, from 9 a m. to 7 p.m. (Stops at 24th & 34th sts.) Miles, 10. Fare, 15 cents.
PORT RICHMOND. Fr. Pier 19. *People's North Shore Ferry.* Miles, 10. Fare 10 cents.
Poughkeepsie. Fr. Pier 39. *Daniel Drew* and *C. Vibbard.* Daily, 8.10 a.m.; W. 24th st., 8.30 a.m. Miles, 76. Fare, $1.00.
Poughkeepsie. Fr. Pier 39. *Mary Powell.* Daily, 3.30 p.m. Miles, 76. Fare, $1.00.
Poughkeepsie. Fr. Pier 35. Propel. *J. L. Hasbrouck* and *D. S. Miller.* Daily, 5 p.m. Miles, 76. Fare, $1.00.
Poughkeepsie. Fr. Pier 43. *J. W. Baldwin* and *Thos. Cornell.* Daily, 4 p.m. Miles. 76. Fare, $1.00.
PROVIDENCE. Fr. Pier 27. *Galatea & Electra.* Daily, 4.30 p.m. Miles, 180. Fare, $3.00.
Red Bank. Fr. Pier 35. *Sea Bird* and *Helen.* Daily, according to tide. Miles, 35. Fare, 50 cents.
Rhinebeck. Fr. Pier 39. *Daniel Drew* and *C. Vibbard.* Daily, 8.10 a.m.; W. 24th st., 8.30 a.m. Miles, 90. Fare, $1.25.
Rhinebeck. Fr. Pier 35. *Andrew Harder* and *Monitor.* Daily, 5 p.m. Miles, 90. Fare, $1.00.
Rockaway Beach. Sea Steamer *Plymouth Rock.* For time of leaving New York, etc., see daily papers.
Rockland Lake. Fr. Pier 34. *Chrystenah.* Daily, 3.30 p.m. (Stops at W. 24th st.) Miles, 35. Fare, 40 cents.
Rondout. Fr. Pier 39. *Mary Powell.* Daily, 3.30 p.m. Miles, 95. Fare, $1.25.
Rondout. Fr. Pier 43. *J. W. Baldwin* and *Thos. Cornell.* Daily, 4 p.m. Miles, 95. Fare, $1.25.
Rossville. Fr. Pier 34. *G. T. Olyphant.* Daily, 3 p.m. Miles, 21. Fare, 25 cents.

Rossville. Fr. Pier 34. *Matteawan.* Sundays only, 9 a.m. Miles, 21. Fare, 25c.
Sailor's Snug Harbor. Fr. Pier 19. *People's North Shore Ferry.* Daily, 6.30, 8.10 a.m., 12 m., 2.00, 4.00, 5.15, 6.30 p.m. Miles, 8. Fare, 10 cents.
SANDY HOOK. Fr. Pier 8. *N. J. Southern R. R. Line Boat.* Miles, 20. Fare, 10 cents.
Saugerties. Fr. Pier 35. *Ansonia.* Tues., Thurs. & Sat., 5.00 p.m. Miles, 101. Fare, $1.00.
Shady Side. From Pier 42. *Pleasant Valley & Fort Lee.* Daily, 10.00 a.m., 2.00, 5.15 p.m. (Stops at 24th st.) Sundays, 10.00 a.m., 2.00, 6.00 p.m. (Stops at 24th & 34th sts.) Miles, 7. Fare, 15 cents.
Sing Sing. Fr. Pier 34. *Adelphi.* Daily, 4 p.m. Miles, 35. Fare, 35 cents.
Smith's Dock. Fr. Pier 42. *New Champion.* Tues., Thurs. & Sat., 6.00 p.m. Miles, 109. Fare, 50 cents.
Smith's Dock. Fr. Pier 35. *Andrew Harder* and *Monitor.* Daily, 5.00 p.m. Miles, 109. Fare, $1.00.
Staatsburg. Fr. Pier 35. *Andrew Harder* and *Monitor.* Daily, 5.00 p.m. Miles, 85. Fare, $1.00.
STAPLETON. Fr. Pier 8. *Sappho.* Daily. Miles, 6. Fare, 5 cents.
Star Landing. Fr. Pier 34. *G. T. Olyphant.* Daily, 3.00 p.m. Miles, 21. Fare, 25 cents.
STONINGTON. Fr. Pier 33. *Stonington* and *Rhode Island.* Daily, 5.00 p.m. Miles, 120. Fare, $2.00.
Stuyvesant. Fr. Pier 35. *Andrew Harder* and *Monitor.* Daily, 5.00 p.m. Miles, 130. Fare $1.00.
Stuyvesant. Fr. Pier 42. *New Champion.* Tues., Thurs. and Sat., 6.00 p.m. Miles, 130. Fare, $50 cents.
Tarrytown (by ferry). Fr. Pier 39. *Daniel Drew & C. Vibbard.* Daily, 8.10 a.m.; W. 24th st., 8.30 a.m. Miles, 28. Fare, 40 cents.
Tarrytown (by ferry). Fr. Pier 34. *Chrystenah.* Daily, 3.30 p.m. (Stops at W. 24th st.) Miles, 28. Fare, 35 cents.
Tarrytown. Fr. Pier 34. *Alexis.* Daily, 5.00 p.m. Miles, 28. Fare, 35 cents.
Tivoli. Fr. Pier 42. *New Champion.* Tues., Thurs. & Sat., 6.00 p.m. Miles, 100. Fare, 50 cents.
Tivoli. Fr. Pier 35. *Andrew Harder* and *Monitor.* Daily, 5 p.m. Miles, 100. Fare, $1.00.
Tivoli. Fr. Pier 35. *Ansonia.* Tues., Thurs. & Sat., 5.00 p.m. Miles, 100. Fare, $1.00.
Tompkins' Cove. Fr. Pier 34. *Chrystenah.* Daily, 3.30 p.m. (Stops at W. 24th st.) Miles, 44. Fare, 45 cents.
Tottenville. Fr. Pier 34. *G. T. Olyphant.* Daily, 3 p.m. Miles, 28. Fare, 25c.
Troy. Fr. Pier 39. (Rail from Albany.) *Daniel Drew* and *C. Vibbard.* Daily, 8.10 a.m.; W. 24th st., 8.30 a.m. Miles, 151. Fare, $2.
Troy. Citizens' Line. Fr. Pier 49. *Thomas Powell* and *Twilight.* Daily, except Saturday, 6 p.m. Sundays also. Miles, 151. Fare, $1.50.
Union Landing. Fr. Pier 34. *G. T. Olyphant.* Daily, 3 p.m. Miles, 20. Fare, 25 cents.
Verplanks Point. Fr. Pier 34. *Adelphi.* Mondays, Wednesdays and Fridays, 3.30 p.m. Miles, 44. Fare, 45 cents.
WEST BRIGHTON. Fr. Pier 19. People's North Shore Ferry. Daily. Miles, 9. Fare 10 cents.
West Park. Fr. Pier 43. *J. W. Baldwin.* Mondays, Wednesdays, and Fridays, 4 p.m. Miles, 82. Fare, $1.25.
West Point. Fr. Pier 39. Albany Day Line. *Daniel Drew* and *C. Vibbard.* Daily, 8.10 a.m.; W. 24th st., 8.30 a.m. Miles, 53 Fare, 75 cents.
West Point. Fr. Pier 39. *Mary Powell.* Daily, 3.30 p.m. Miles, 53. Fare, 75c.
West Point. Fr. Pier 42. *New Champion.* Tuesdays and Thursdays, 6 p.m. Miles, 53. Fare, 50 cents.
West Point. Steamer *Long Branch.* Fr. Fulton st., Brooklyn, 8 a.m.; W. 10th st., 8.30 a.m.; W. 24th st., 9 a.m. Sundays only. Miles, 53. Fare, $1.
Yonkers. Fr. Pier 34. *Chrystenah.* Daily, 3.30 p.m. (Stops at W. 24th st.) Miles, 17. Fare, 20 cents.
Yonkers. Fr. Pier 34. *Adelphi.* Daily, 4 p.m. Miles 17. Fare, 20 cents.
Yonkers. Fr. Pier 34. *Alexis.* Daily, 5 p.m. Miles, 17. Fare, 20 cents.

CITY OF NEW YORK.

Yonkers. Str. *Long Branch.* Fr. Fulton st., Brooklyn, 8 a.m.; W. 10th st., 8.30 a.m.; W. 24th st., 9 a.m. Sundays only. Miles, 17. Fare, 25 cents.

FROM EAST RIVER PIERS.

ASTORIA and Harlem. Fr. Pier 24. *Sylvan Grove, Glen, Dell* and *Stream.* Miles, 6. Fare, 10 cents.

ASTORIA. Fr. Pier 22. *Morrisania, Shady Side* and *Harlem.* Daily. Miles, 6. Fare, 10 cents.

Baylis Dock. Fr. Pier 24. *Seawanhaka.* Daily, 4 p.m. (Stops at 33d st.) Miles, 14. Fare, 10 cents.

BRIDGEPORT. Fr. Pier 35. *Bridgeport.* Daily, 11.30 a.m. Miles, 65. Fare, $1.

CITY ISLAND. Fr. Pier 24. *Seawanhaka.* Sundays only, 9 a.m.; E. Ninth st., 9.05 a.m.; E. 33d st., 9.15 a.m. Miles 19. Fare 50 cents.

Deep River. Fr. Pier 24. *State of New York* and *City of Hartford.* Dai y, 4 p.m. Miles, 104. Fare, $1.75.

ELM PARK. Fr. Pier 1. *Staten Island.* North Shore Ferry. Sundays only. Every town from 8.30 a.m. to 4.30 p.m. Miles, 11. Fare, 10 cents.

Essex. Fr. Pier 24. *State of New York* and *City of Hartford.* Daily, 4 p.m. Miles, 100. Fare, $1.75.

Glastenbury. Fr. Pier 24. *State of New York* and *City of Hartford.* Daily, 4 p.m. Miles, 152. Fare, $1.75.

Glen Cove. Fr. Pier 24. *Seawanhaka.* Daily, 4 p.m, (Stops at 33d st.) Miles, 23. Fare, 40 cents.

Glen Wood. Fr. Pier 24. *Seawanhaka.* Daily, 4 p.m. (Stops at 33d st.) Miles, 28. Fare, 40 cents.

Goodspeed. Fr. Pier 24. *State of New York* and *City of Hartford.* Daily, 4 p.m. Miles, 110. Fare, $1.75.

Great Neck. Fr. Pier 24. *Seawanhaka.* Daily, 4 p.m. (Stops at 33d st.) Miles, 16. Fare, 35 cents.

Greenport. Fr. Pier 25. *W. W. Coit.* Tuesdays, Thursdays and Saturdays, 5 p.m. Miles, 125. Fare, $1.

HARLEM. Fr. Pier 24. *Sylvan Grove, Glen, Dell* and *Stream.* Daily. Miles, 9. Fare, 10 cents.

Hartford. Fr. Pier 24. *State of New York* and *City of Hartford.* Daily, 4 p.m. Miles, 160. Fare, $1.75.

High Bridge. Fr. Harlem. Daily, every half hour. Sundays also. Connecting with boats from Pier 24. E. R, and from Pier 22, E. R. Fare, 10 cents.

Lyme. Fr. Pier 24. *State of New York* and *Ci y of Hartford.* Daily, 4 p.m. Miles, 98. Fare, $1.75.

Middle Haddam. Fr. Pier 24. *State of New York* and *City of Hartford.* Daily, 4 p.m. Miles 125. Fare, $1.75.

Middletown. Fr. Pier 24. *State of New York* and *City of Hartford.* Daily, 4 p.m. Miles, 131. Fare, $1.75.

MORRISANIA. Fr. Pier 22. *Morrisania, Shady Side* and *Harlem.* Daily. Miles, 9. Fare, 10 cents.

New Bedford. Fr. Pier 39. New Bedford and New York S. S. Co. *City of Fitchburg* and *City of New Bedford.* Daily, 5 p.m. Miles, 185. Fare, $3.

NEW BRIGHTON. Fr. Pier 1. Staten Island North Shore Ferry. Miles, 7. Fare, 10 cents.

NEW HAVEN. Fr. Pier 25. *Northam* and *Continental.* Daily, 3 and 11 p.m. Miles, 76. Fare, $1.25.

New Suffolk. Fr. Pier 25. *W. W. Coit.* To New Suffolk from Sag Harbor, on Monday. Miles, 140. Fare, $1.00.

Orient. Fr. Pier 25. *W. W. Coit.* Tuesday, Thursday and Saturday, 5 p.m. Miles, 120. Fare, $1.00.

Portland, Conn. Fr. Pier 24. *State of New York* and *City of Hartford.* Daily, 4 p.m. Miles, 132. Fare, $1.75.

PORT RICHMOND. Fr. Pier 1. Staten Island North Shore Ferry.

Port Washington, L. I. Fr. Pier 24. *Seawanhaka* (connects by stage). Daily, 4 p.m. Stops at 33d st. each way. Miles, 28. Fare, 50 cents.

CITY OF NEW YORK.

RANDALL'S ISLAND. Fr. Pier 22. Morrisania boat. Daily, 10.45 a.m. Fare, 10 cents.

RANDALL'S ISLAND. Fr. Pier 24. Harlem boat. Daily, 10.40 a.m. Fare, 10 cents.

Roslyn. Fr. Pier 24. *Seawanhaka*. Daily, 4 p.m. (Stops at 33d st.) Miles, 30. Fare, 40 cents.

Sag Harbor. Fr. Pier 25. *W. W. Coit*. Tuesday, Thursday and Saturday. 5 p.m. Miles. 140. Fare, $1.00.

Sailors' Snug Harbor. Fr. Pier 1. Staten Island North Shore Ferry. Miles, 8. Fare, 10 cents.

Sands Point. Fr. Pier 24. *Seawanhaka*. Daily, 4 p.m., (stops at 33d st). Sundays (50 cents), 9 a.m. (stops at 9th and 33d sts.) Miles, 26. Fare, 40c.

Saybrook. Fr. Pier 24. *State of New York* and *City of Hartford*. Daily, 4 p.m. Miles. 96. Fare, $1.50.

Sea Cliff Grove. Fr. Pier 24. *Seawanhaka*. Daily, 4 p.m. (Stops at 33d st.) Miles, 20. Fare, 40 cents.

Shelter Island Fr. Pier 25. *W. W. Coit*. Tuesday, Thursday and Saturday. 5 p.m. Miles, 140. Fare, $1.00.

South Norwalk. Fr. Pier 37. *Americus*. Daily, 2.45 p.m.; E. 33d st., 3 p.m. Miles, 49. Fare, 35 cents.

STAPLETON. Fr. Pier 1. Staten Island Railroad Ferry. Daily. Miles, 6. Fare, 10 cents.

TOMPKINSVILLE. Fr. Pier 1. Staten Island Railroad Ferry. Daily. Miles, 5. Fare, 10 cents.

VANDERBILT LANDING. Fr. Pier 1. Staten Island Railroad Ferry. Daily, Miles, 7. Fare. 10 cents.

WEST BRIGHTON. Fr. Pier 1. Staten Island North Shore Ferry. Daily. Miles, 9. Fare, 10 Cents.

YORKVILLE, 84th st. Fr. Pier 24. Harlem boats. Daily. Miles, 6. Fare, 10 cents.

OCEAN STEAMERS—FOREIGN PORTS.

M., monthly; S.M., semi-monthly; T.M., tri-monthly; W., weekly; S.W., semi-weekly; T.W., tri-weekly; D., daily.

Destination.	*Time.*	*Pier.*	*Offices.*
Antwerp and Rotterdam	M	Jersey City, (Long Dock.)	Funch, Edye & Co., 27 S. William st.
Antwerp	S.M.	53 N. R.	Red Star Line, 42 Broad st.
Aspinwall	S.M.	42 N. R.	Pacific Mail S. S. Co., Pier 42 N. R.
Bermuda	S.M.	12 N. R.	A. E. Outerbridge, 29 Broadway.
Brazil and Porto Rico	M	Watson's Pr. B'klyn	J. S. Tucker & Co., 54 Pine st.
Bremen, via Southampton	W	Third street, Hoboken	North German Lloyd, 2 Bowling Gr.
Bristol, England	S.M.	18 E. R.	W. D. Morgan, 10 South st.
China and Japan, via San Francisco	S.M.	42 N. R.	Pacific Mail S. S. Co., Pier 42 N. R.
Glasgow, via Londonderry	W	20 N. R.	Anchor Line, 7 Bowling Green.
Glasgow, via Belfast	S.M.	42 N. R.	Austin, Baldwin & Co., 72 B'way.
Halifax, N. S.	T.M.	10 N. R.	Clark & Seaman, 86 West st.
Hamburg, via Plymouth and Cherbourg	W	Third street, Hoboken	C. B. Richard & Boas, 61 B'way.
Havana and Mexico	S.M.	3 N. R.	F. Alexandre & Sons, 33 Broadway.
Havana	S.M.	13 N. R.	W. P. Clyde & Co., 6 Bowling Green.
Havre and Brest, via Plymouth	W	Barrow st.	Louis de Babian, 55 Broadway.
Hayti, Jamaica, and New Grenada	S.M.	51 N. R.	Pim, Forwood & Co., 56 Wall st.
Hull, via Southampton	S.M.	53 N. R.	Chas. L. Wright & Co., 56 South st.
Liverpool, via Queenstown	W	Grand st., Jersey City.	Cunard Line, 4 Bowling Green.
Liverpool, via Queenstown	T.M.	45 N. R.	Inman Line, 15 Broadway.
Liverpool, via Queenstown	S.M.	52 N. R.	White Star Line, 37 Broadway.
Liverpool, via Queenstown	S.M.	44 or 47 N.R.	National Line, 69 Broadway.
Liverpool, via Queenstown	T.M.	46 N. R.	Williams & Guion, 29 Broadway.
London	M	47 N. R.	F. W. J. Hurst, 59 Broadway.
London, Bordeaux, and Mediterranean	S.M.	20 N. R.	Anchor Line, 7 Bowling Green.
Nassau	M	16 E. R.	Murray, Ferry & Co., 62 South st.
St. Domingo and Samana		12 N. R.	W. P. Clyde & Co., 6 Bowling Green.
St. Johns, N. F.	T.M.	10 N. R.	Clark & Seaman, 86 West st.
St. Thomas and Venezuela		20 E. R.	C. H. Mallory & Co., 153 Maiden La.

DOMESTIC PORTS.

Destination.	*Time.*	*Pier.*	*Offices.*
Alexandria, Va., and Washington, D. C.	W	41 E. R.	J. L. Roome, Jr., 226 South st.
Charleston, S. C.	S.W.	29 N. R.	J. W. Quintard & Co., 177 West st.
Fernandina, Fla., and Port Royal, S. C.	W	20 E. R.	C. H. Mallory & Co., 153 Maiden La.
Galveston, Texas, via Key West	W	20 E. R.	C. H. Mallory & Co., 153 Maiden La.
New Orleans	W	36 N. R.	Morgan's Line, Pier 36 N. R.
New Orleans	W	10 N. R.	Clark & Seaman, 86 West st.
Philadelphia	D	33 E. R.	James Hand, Pier 33 E. R.
Portland, Me.	S.W.	38 E. R.	J. F. Ames, Pier 38 E. R.
Richmond, Portsmouth, Norfolk and City Point, Va., and Lewes, Del.	T.W.	37 N. R.	W. L. McCready, 197 Greenwich st.
San Francisco, via Panama	S.M.	42 N. R.	Pacific Mail S. S. Co., Pier 42 N. R.
Savannah, Ga.	S.W.	43 N. R.	W. R. Garrison, 5 Bowling Green.
Savannah, Ga.	W	16 E. R.	Murray, Ferris & Co., 62 South st.
Wilmington, Del.	T.W.	14 E. R.	Abiel Abbot, 53 South st.
Wilmington, N. C.	W	13 N. R.	W. P. Clyde, 6 Bowling Green.

Equitable Life Insurance Company's Building,

Broadway and Cedar Street.

The new Tribune Building.

WALLING'S

NEW STREET DIRECTORY

OF NEW YORK,

SHOWING THE STREETS, AVENUES, LANES, COURTS, PLACES, ETC., TOGETHER WITH THE NUMBERINGS AT THE STREET CROSSINGS,

Prepared from the Official Records.

EXPLANATION.

The streets are given in alphabetical order; those streets which are divided into east and west being placed under E. and W.

Numbers are given at each intersection, so far as numbers have been assigned. The number given is the lowest one on either corner.

ABBREVIATIONS.

al.	Alley	fr.	From	N.	North	S.	South
av.	Avenue	E. R.	East River	N. R.	North River	sl.	Slip
bet.	Between	gr.	Green	pk.	Park	sq.	Square
c.	Corner	la.	Lane	r.	Rear	ter.	Terrace
ct.	Court	m'k't	Market	pl.	Place	W.	West

Abattoir pl. foot of W. 39th st.

Abingdon pl. W. 12th, bet 8th av & Greenwich.

Abingdon sq. Bleecker fr Bank to 8th av, from 1 to 10 8th av, & fr 585 to 609 Hudson.

Ackerman pl. New Chambers, bet Chatham & William.

Albany, fr 122 Greenwich, W. to N. R.
1 Greenwich
13 Washington
23 West

Albion pl. fr 56 to 78 E 4th

Allen, fr 104 Division, N. to E. Houston
1 Division
12 Canal
39 Hester
66 Grand
85 Broome
115 Delancey
145 Rivington
177 Stanton
213 E. Houston

Amity, fr 681 B'way to 6th av.
1 Broadway
6 Mercer
24 Greene
40 Wooster
60 Laurens
76 Thompson
92 Sullivan
111 Macdougal
141 6th av.

Amity pl. r 216 Wooster

Amity pl. Laurens st, bet Bleecker & Amity

Amity la. r 190 Greene

Ann, fr 222 B'w'y E. to Gold
1 Park Row
2 Broadway
19 Theatre al.
31 Nassau
69 William
91 Gold

Ashland pl. Perry street, bet Greenwich av & Waverly pl.

Astor pl. fr 744 B'way, E. to 4th av.
— Broadway
— Lafayette pl.
— Eighth
— Fourth av.

Attorney, fr 236 Division, N to E. Houston
1 Division
17 Grand
44 Broome
71 Delancey
111 Rivington
143 Stanton
176 E. Houston

Av. A, fr 230 E. Houston, N. to E. R.
2 E. Houston
5 First
21 Second

3 Mechanic pl.
37 Third
53 E Fourth
71 Fifth
88 Sixth
101 Seventh
117 St. Mark's pl.
129 Ninth
143 E. 10th
(101–143: Tompkins sq.)
154 E. 11th
170 E. 12th
186 E. 13th
205 E. 14th
221 E. 15th
237 E. 16th
253 E. 17th
269 E. 18th
285 E. 19th
299 E. 20th
319 E. 21st
— E. 22d
487 E. 23d
497 E. 24th

Av. B, fr 296 E. Houston, N. to E. R.
1 E. Houston
15 Second
35 Third
53 E. 4th
73 Fifth
91 Sixth
109 Seventh
127 Eighth
143 Ninth
157 E. 10th
(109–157: Tompkins sq.)
173 E. 11th
193 E. 12th
209 E. 13th
236 E. 14th
257 E. 15th
273 E. 16th
291 E. 17th
— E. 18th
— E. 19th
— E. 20th

Av. C, fr 358 E. Houston, N. to E. R.
1 E. Houston
8 Second
28 Third
44 E. 4th
60 Fifth
80 Sixth
101 Seventh
121 Eighth
139 Ninth
157 E. 10th
177 E. 11th
195 E. 12th
211 E. 13th
— E. 14th
— E. 15th
— E. 16th
— E. 17th
— E. 18th
(— E. 14th to — E. 18th: Tompkins sq.)

Av. D, fr 422 E. Houston, N. to E. R.
2 E. Houston
1 Second
15 Third
33 E. 4th
55 Fifth
73 Sixth
91 Seventh
109 Eighth
127 Ninth
143 E. 10th
— E. 11th
— E. 12th
— E. 13th
— E. 14th
— E. 15th
— E. 16th

Bank, fr 85 Gr'nwich av, W. to N. R.
1 Greenwich av.
14 Waverley pl.
51 W. 4th
82 Bleecker
90 Hudson
98 Greenwich
138 Washington
149 Nyack pl.
166 West
200 Thirteenth av.

Barclay, fr 229 B'way, W. to N. R.
1 Broadway
23 Church
53 College pl.
73 Greenwich
87 Washington
105 West

Barrow, fr 59 W. Wash'gton pl. W. to N. R.
1 W Wash. pl.
2 W. 4th
28 Bleecker
58 Bedford
73 Commerce
84 Hudson
100 Greenwich
112 Washington
142 West

Batavia, fr 78 Roosevelt, E. to James
1 Roosevelt
7 NewChambers
24 James

Battery pl. fr 1 B'way, W. to N. R.
1 Broadway
4 Greenwich
7 Washington
12 West

Baxter, fr 136 Chatham, N. to Grand
1 Chatham
27 Park
30 Worth
46 Leonard
64 Franklin
71 Bayard
82 White
102 Walker
104 Canal
128 Hester
155 Grand

Bayard, fr 82 Division, W. to Baxter
1 Division
2 Forsyth
17 Christie
37 Bowery
52 Elizabeth
73 Mott
91 Mulberry
107 Baxter

Beach, fr 134 W. B'way, W. to N. R.
1 W. B'way
6 St. John's la.
12 Varick
42 Hudson
51 Collister
62 Greenwich
65 Washington
79 West

Beaver, fr 8 Broadway, E. to Pearl
1 Broadway
9 New
31 Broad
57 William
74 Hanover
95 Pearl

Bedford, fr 18 W. Houston, N. to Christopher
1 W. Houston
22 Downing
30 Carmine
44 Leroy
56 Morton
74 Commerce
80 Barrow
96 Grove
110 Christopher

Beekman, fr 34 Park row, S. E. to E. R.
1 Park row
3 Theatre al.
9 Nassau
37 William
61 Gold
89 Cliff
103 Pearl
119 Water
125 Front
140 South

Belvidere pl. W. 30th, bet 9th & 10th avs.

Benson, fr 109 Leonard, N.

Bethune, fr 782 Greenwich, W. to N. R.
1 Greenwich
31 Washington
61 West
— Thirteenth av.

Bible House, on 8th & 9th sts. & Third & Fourth avs.

Billing's Row, W. 50th st. bet Eighth & Ninth avs.

Birmingham, fr 84 Henry, S. to 137 Madison

Bishop's la. fr 174 Chambers, S. to Warren

Bleecker, fr 318 Bowery, W. & N. to Eighth av.
1 Bowery
10 Elizabeth
30 Mott
52 Mulberry
64 Crosby
73 Broadway
88 Mercer
101 Greene
117 Wooster
133 Laurens
147 Thompson
167 Sullivan
185 Macdougal
202 Hancock
205 Minetta
210 Downing
226 Carmine
238 Leroy
247 Cornelia
256 Morton
265 Jones
272 Commerce
280 Barrow
299 Grove
310 Christopher
328 W. 10th
346 Charles
364 Perry
382 W. 11th
396 Bank
401 Eighth av.

Bloomingdale road, B'way, N. to Harlem

Bond, fr 658 B'way E. to Bowery

Boorman pl. W. 33d, bet Eighth & Ninth avs.

Boorman ter. W. 32d, bet Eighth & Ninth avs.

Boulevard, fr W. 59th & Eighth av. to W. 70th & Tenth av., thence to W. 106th & Bloomingdale road, thence to W. 155th & Eleventh av.

Bowery, fr 210 Chatham, N. to 4th av.
1 Division
— Catharine
2 Doyers
18 Pell
29 Bayard
61 Canal
90 Hester
122 Grand
145 Broome
181 Delancey
188½ Spring
213 Rivington
230½ Prince
245 Stanton
284 E. Houston
303 First
318 Bleecker
321 Second
328 Bond
343 Third
346 Gt. Jones
361 E. 4th
379 Fifth
395 Sixth
402 Fourth av.

Bowling Green, fr 2 Whitehall, W. to State

Brevoort pl. E. 10th st. bet. University pl. & B'way

Bridge, fr 15 State, E. to Broad
1 State
11 Whitehall
40 Broad

Broad, fr 21 Wall, S. to E. R.
1 Wall
28 Exchange pl.
68 Beaver,
72 Marketfield
81 S. William
88 Stone
98 Bridge
100 Pearl
108 Water
122 Front
142 South

Broadway, fr 1 Battery pl. N. to Bloomingdale road
1 Battery pl.
2 Marketfield
8 Beaver
25 Morris
55 Exchange al.
56 Exchange pl.
73 Rector
86 Wall
106 Pine
111 Thames
124 Cedar
145 Liberty
171 Cortlandt
172 Maiden la.
191 John
192 Dey
210 Fulton
222 Ann
— Vesey
229 Barclay
237 Park pl.
247 Murray
260 Warren
271 Chambers
287 Reade
302 Duane
318 Pearl
331 Worth
344 Catharine la.
347 Leonard
363 Franklin
379 White
399 Walker
413 Lispenard
417 Canal
432 Howard
458 Grand
486 Broome
527 Spring
567 Prince
609 W. and E. Houston
640 Bleecker
658 Bond
681 Amity
682 Gt. Jones
696 W. & E. 4th
713 Washington pl.
727 Waverley pl.
744 Astor pl.
755 Clinton pl.
754 8th
769 9th
784 E. 10th
801 W. 11th
819 E. 12th
835 E. 13th
851 E. 14th
— E. 15th
— E. 16th
857 E. 17th
871 E. 18th
887 E. 19th
901 E. 20th
919 E. 21st
937 E. 22d
956 E. 23d
957 Fifth av.
1101 W. 24th
1117 W. 25th
1135 W. 26th
1155 W. 27th
1183 W. 28th
1203 W. 29th
1227 W. 30th
1251 W. 31st
1273 W. 32d
1280 W. 33d
1300 Sixth av.
1308 W. 34th
1314 W. 35th
1348 W. 36th
1364 W. 37th
1380 W. 38th
1400 W. 39th
1418 W. 40th
1438 W. 41st
1425 W. 42d
1439 W. 43d
— W. 44th
— Seventh av.
— W. 45th
1501 W. 46th
1516 W. 47th
1573 W. 48th
1588 W. 49th
1407 W. 50th
— W. 51st
1399 W. 52d
1415 W. 53d

B'dway al. fr 153 E. 26th, N. to E. 27th

Broome, fr E. R. W. to Hudson
1 East
3 Tompkins
17 Mangin
32 Goerck
50 Lewis
66 Cannon
82 Columbia
97 Sheriff
113 Willett
127 Pitt
143 Ridge
160 Attorney
177 Clinton
194 Suffolk
209 Norfolk
225 Essex
241 Ludlow
258 Orchard
273 Allen
289 Eldridge
304 Forsyth
321 Chrystie
335 Bowery
353 Elizabeth
369 Mott
385 Mulberry
395 Centre M'k'tpl.
404 Marion
403 Centre
411 Elm
427 Crosby
441 Broadway
452 Mercer
467 Greene
481 Wooster
499 Laurens
515 Thompson
532 Sullivan
538 Clarke
562 Varick
588 Hudson

Burling sl. fr 234 Pearl, S. E. to E. R
1 Pearl
10 Water
24 Front
42 South

Camden pl. E. 11th, bet avs B and C

Canal, fr 179 E. B'way, W. to N. R.
1 E Broadway
24 Rutgers
26 Division
37 Ludlow
53 Orchard
70 Allen
84 Eldridge
104 Forsyth
122 Chrystie
138 Bowery
162 Elizabeth
182 Mott
201 Mulberry
219 Baxter
237 Centre
249 Elm
270 Cortland al.
286 Broadway
311 Mercer
331 Greene
346 Church
355 Wooster
375 Laurens
384 W. Broadway
395 Thompson
398 Laight
415 Sullivan
429 Varick
428 Vestry
468 Hudson
484 Watts
486 Renwick
500 Greenwich
520 Hoboken
520 Washington
— West

Cannon, fr 540 Grand, N. to E. Houston
1 Grand
19 Broome
43 Delancey
77 Rivington
105 Stanton
137 E. Houston

Carlisle, fr 112 Greenwich, W. to N. R.
1 Greenwich
8 Washington
16 West

Carmine. fr 1 Sixth av. W. to Varick
1 Sixth av.
2 Minetta la.
15 Bleecker
49 Bedford
81 Varick

Caroline, fr 211 Duane, N. to Jay

Carroll pl. Bleecker st bet Laurens and Thompson

Catharine, fr Bowery, S. to Cherry
1 Division
2 Chatham sq.
9 E. Broadway
23 Henry
41 Madison
59 Monroe
68 Oak
73 Hamilton
100 Cherry

Catharine la. fr 56 Elm, W. to 344 Broadway

Catharine m'k't, foot of Catharine

Catharine sl. fr 115 Cherry, S. E. R.
1 Cherry
10 Water
24 South

Cedar, fr 181 Pearl, W. to N. R.
1 Pearl
39 William
64 Nassau
89 Broadway
95 Temple
103 Trinity pl.
127 Greenwich
143 Washington
159 West

Centre, fr the Park, N. to Broome
1 Tryon row
12 Chambers
14 City Hall pl.
22 Reade
31 Duane
36 Park st.
50 Pearl
70 Worth
90 Leonard
110 Franklin
132 White
150 Walker
156 Canal
182 Hester
201 Howard
223 Grand
257 Broome

Centre m'k't, Centre, c. Grand

Centre m'k't, pl. fr 172 Grand, N. to Broome

Chambers, fr 66 Chatham, W to N. R.
1 Chatham
15 City Hall pl.
23 Centre
69 Broadway
99 Church
132 College pl.
131 W. Broadway
139 Hudson
171 Greenwich
174 Bishop's la.
182 Washington
205 West

Charles fr 37 Greenwich av, W. to N. R.
1 Greenwich av.
17 Waverly pl.
53 W. 4th
84 Bleecker
114 Hudson
125 Greenwich
145 Washington
172 West

Charles la. fr 694 Washington, W. to West

Charlton, fr 29 Macdougal, W to N. R.
1 Macdougal
55 Varick
89 Hudson

121 Greenwich
119 Washington
139 West

Chatham, fr City Hall sq. E. to Chatham sq.
1 Frankfort
26 Tryon row
49 N. William
66 Chambers
67 New Chambers
68 Duane
124 Pearl
136 Baxter
147 Roosevelt
156 Mulberry
175 James
180 Mott
191 New Bowery
207 E. Broadway
208 Doyers
210 Bowery

Chatham sq. fr 2 Catharine to E. Broadway

Chelsea Cottages, W. 24th, bet 9th and 10th avs.

Cherry, fr 1 Dover, E. to E. R.
1 Dover
8 Franklin sq.
34 W. Gotham pl.
38 E. Gotham pl.
45 Roosevelt
74 New Chambers
75 James
77 James sl.
98 Oliver
114 Catharine
115 Catharine sl.
164 Market
196 Mechanic al.
208 Pike
228 Pelham
254 Rutgers
280 Jefferson
313 Clinton
348 Montgomery
373 Gouverneur
383 Scammel
438 Jackson
486 Corlears
525 East

Chestnut, fr 8 Oak, N. to Madison
1 Oak
6 New Bowery
20 New Chambers
28 Madison

Christopher, fr 5 Greenwich av., W. to N. R.
1 Greenwich av.
12 Gay
28 Waverley pl.
63 W. 4th
91 Bleecker
126 Bedford
129 Hudson
143 Greenwich
151 Washington
175 Weehawken
177 West

Chrystie, fr 44 Division, N. to E. Houston
1 Division
8 Bayard
42 Canal
71 Hester
99 Grand
123 Broome
151 Delancey
178 Rivington
205 Stanton
232 E. Houston

Church, fr 189 Fulton, N. to Canal
1 Fulton
16 Vesey
24 Barclay
36 Park pl.
56 Murray
64 Warren
86 Chambers
94 Reade
111 Duane
126 Thomas
140 Worth
160 Leonard
174 Franklin
192 White
208 Walker
222 Lispenard
236 Canal

City Hall pl. fr 15 Chambers, N. E. to Pearl
1 Chambers
2 Centre
9 Reade
10 Duane
40 Pearl

City Hall sq. "the space bet Tryon row & Ann st."

Clarke, fr 538 Broome, N. to Spring
1 Broome
13 Dominick
31 Spring

Clarkson, fr 225 Varick, W. to N. R.
1 Varick
24 Hudson
53 Greenwich
60 Washington
81 West

Cliff, fr 101 John, N. E. to Hague
1 John
34 Fulton
54 Beekman
72 Ferry
101 Frankfort
108 Hague

Clinton, fr 295 E. Houston, S. to E. R.
1 E. Houston
29 Stanton
48 E. Clinton pl.
77 Rivington
97 Clinton al.
104 Delancey
137 Broome
163 Grand
191 { Hester / Division }
197 E. Broadway
207 Henry
217 Madison
232 Monroe
249 Cherry
255 Water
— South

Clinton al. fr 97 Clinton to 104 Suffolk

Clinton ct. fr 120 Clinton pl.

Clinton Hall, Astor pl.

Clinton mkt. West, c Canal

Clinton pl. fr 755 B'way, W to Sixth av.
1 Broadway
10 Mercer
26 Greene
41 University pl.
65 Fifth av.
96 Macdougal
120 Clinton ct.
137 Sixth av.

Coenties' al. fr 73 Pearl, N W. to Stone

Coenties' sl. fr 66 Pearl, S. to E. R.
1 Pearl
6 Water
18 Front
28 South

College pl. fr 53 Barclay, N. to Chambers
1 Barclay
3 Park pl.
4 Robinson
11 Murray
20 Warren
— Chambers

Collester, fr 51 Beach, N. to Laight
1 Beach
— Hubert
— Laight

Columbia, fr 520 Grand, N. to E. Houston
1 Grand
19 Broome
46 Delancey
72 Rivington
101 Stanton
129 E. Houston

Columbia pl. 386 Eighth st.

Commerce, fr 272 Bleecker, W. to Barrow.
1 Bleecker
27 Bedford
41 Barrow

Congress, from 177 W. Houston, S. to King

Congress pl. opposite 3 Congress st.

Cooper Un. on Eighth st. & 3d & 4th avs.

Corlears, fr 587 Grand, S. to E.R.
1 Grand
10 Monroe
28 Cherry
38 Water
— Front
— South

Cornelia, fr 160 W. 4th, W. to Bleecker

Cortlandt. fr 171 B'way, W. to N. R.
1 Broadway
51 Greenwich
63 Washington
81 West

Cortlandt al. fr 270 Canal, S. to Franklin
1 Canal
— Walker
— White
— Franklin

Cottage pl. Hancock st.

Cottage pl. Third st, bet avs B and C

Crosby, fr 28 Howard, N. to Bleecker
1 Howard
21 Grand
43 Broome
73 Spring
105 Prince
127 Jersey
140 E. Houston
— Bleecker

Cuyler's al. fr 28 South, W. to Water

Davies pl. W. 36th, bet B'way & Sixth av.

Decatur pl. Seventh st. fr 96 to 114

Delancey, fr 181 Bowery, E. to E. R.
1 Bowery
18 Chrystie
34 Forsyth
53 Eldridge
66 Allen
84 Orchard
97 Ludlow
113 Essex
131 Norfolk
147 Suffolk
164 Clinton
179 Attorney
195 Ridge
213 Pitt
229 Willett
245 Sheriff
263 Columbia
285 Cannon
302 Lewis
320 Goerck
328 Mangin
339 Tompkins
346 East

Depau pl. 185 & 187 Thompson

Depau row, 154 to 158 Bleecker.

Depeyster, fr 139 Water, S. to E. R.
1 Water
14 Front
39 South

Desbrosses, fr 195 Hudson, W. to N. R.
1 Hudson
22 Greenwich
30 Washington
43 West

Dey, fr 192 B'way W. to N. R.
1 Broadway
60 Greenwich
71 Washington
87 West

Division, fr 1 Bowery, E. to Grand
2 Bowery
1 Catharine
44 Chrystie
68 Forsyth
82 Bayard
61 Market
86 Eldridge
104 Allen
107 Pike
124 Orchard
143 Canal
144 Ludlow
162 Essex
180 Norfolk
179 Jefferson
202 Suffolk
216½ Hester
218 Clinton
236 Attorney
247 Montgomery
254 Ridge
276 Pitt
275 Gouverneur
280 Grand

Dixon's row, W. 110th, from Bloomingdale to Ninth av.

Dominick, fr 13 Clarke, W. to Hudson
1 Clarke
22 Varick
51 Hudson

Donovan's la. r 474 Pearl

Dover, fr 3[illegible] Pearl, S. to E. R.
1 Cherry
2 Pearl
11 Water
20 Front
44 South

Downing, f[illegible] 210 Bleecker, W to Varick
1 Bleecker
16 Jackson pl.
32 Bedford
70 Varick

Doyers, fr 20[illegible] Chatham, W. and N. to Pell

Dry Dock, f[illegible] 243 E. 10th, N to E. 12th
1 E. 10th
10 E 11th
21 E 12th

Duane, fr 4[illegible] Rose, W. to N. R.
1 Rose
13 North William
14 New Chambers
18 Chatham
22 Reade
29 City Hall pl.
38 Centre
39 Park
59 Elm
90 Broadway
124 Church
149 W. Broadway
162 Hudson
169 Staple
190 Greenwich
200 Washington
211 Caroline
220 West

Duncomb pl. E. 128th, f[illegible] Second to Third avs.

Dunham pl. r. 140 W. 33d

Dutch, fr 4[illegible] John, N. to Fulton

East, fr 755 Water, E. to Rivington
— Water
— Cherry
— Grand
— Broome
20 Delancey
44 Rivington

E. Bro'dway, fr 207 Chatham, E. to Grand
1 Chatham sq.
15 Catharine
73 Market
116 Pike
162 Rutgers
179 Canal
189 Jefferson
219 Clinton
259 Montgomery
287 Gouverneur
299 Scammel
311 Grand

East Clinton pl. r. 50 Clinton

East Gotham pl. from 138 Cherry

East Houston, from 609 Broadway, E. to E. R.
1 Broadway
19 Crosby
35 Mulberry
55 Mott
71 Elizabeth
89 Bowery
117 Chrystie
118 Second av.
133 Forsyth
151 Eldridge
164 First av
165 Allen
185 Orchard
203 Ludlow
227 Essex
230 Avenue A
243 Norfolk
267 Suffolk
295 Clinton
296 Avenue B
317 Attorney
335 Ridge
357 Pitt
358 Avenue C
379 Willett
401 Sheriff
421 Columbia
442 Avenue D
444 Manhattan
443 Cannon
466 Lewis
483 Goerck
509 Mangin
531 Tompkins
547 East

East pl. r 214 3d

E. 4th, fr 696 Broadway, E. to E. R.
1 Broadway
15 Lafayette pl.
45 Bowery
84 Second av.
131 First av.
180 Avenue A
242 Avenue B
304 Avenue C
362 Avenue D
392 Lewis
— Mangin
— Tompkins

E. 10th, fr 33 Fifth av, E. to E. R.
2 Fifth av.
21 University pl.
62 Broadway
76 Fourth av.
100 Third av.
128 Stuyvesant
203 Second av.
246 First av.
291 Avenue A
345 Avenue B
397 Avenue C
422 Knapp's pl.
423 Dry Dock
450 Avenue D

E. 11th, fr 91 Fourth av. E. to E. R.
1 Fourth av.
26 Third av.
62 Second av.
113 First av.
156 Avenue A
203 Avenue B
261 Avenue C
293 Dry Dock
— Avenue D

E. 12th, fr 51 Fifth av. E. to E. R.
1 Fifth av.
31 University pl.
55 Broadway
100 Fourth av.
200 Third av.
300 Second av
401 First av.
500 Avenue A
600 Avenue B
700 Avenue C
730 Dry Dock
800 Avenue D

E. 13th, fr 61 Fifth av. E. to E. R.
1 Fifth av.
35 University pl.
65 Broadway
100 Fourth av.
200 Third av.
300 Second av
400 First av.
500 Avenue A
600 Anenue B
700 Avenue C
800 Avenue D

E. 14th, fr 69 Fifth av., E. to E. R.
1 Fifth av.
31 Union pl.
— University pl.
55 Broadway
100 Fourth av.
200 Third av.
300 Second av.
401 First av.
500 Avenue A
600 Avenue B
700 Avenue C
800 Avenue D

E. 15th, fr 71 Fifth av. E. to E. R.
1 Fifth av.
29 Union pl.
100 Fourth av.
122 Irving pl.
200 Third av.
— Rutherford pl.
300 Second av.
225 Livingston pl.
400 First av.
500 Avenue A
600 Avenue B
700 Avenue C
800 Avenue D

E. 16th, fr. 81 Fifth av. E. to E. R.
1 Fifth av.
24 Broadway
105 Fourth av.
122 Irving pl.
200 Third av.
226 Rutherford pl.
— Second av.
320 Livingston pl.
400 First av.
500 Avenue A
600 Avenue B
— Avenue C
— Avenue D

E. 17th, fr 95 Fifth av, E. to E. R.
1 Fifth av.
25 Broadway
100 Fourth av.
124 Irving pl.
200 Third av.
224 Rutherford pl.
301 Second av.
330 Livingston pl.
400 First av.
500 Avenue A
600 Avenue B
— Avenue C
— Avenue D

E. 18th, fr 107 Fifth av, E. to E. R.
2 Fifth av.
19 Broadway
100 Fourth av.
126 Irving pl.
200 Third av.
300 Second av.
400 First av.
500 Avenue A
600 Avenue B
700 Avenue C

E. 19th, fr 119 Fifth av, E. to E. R.
1 Fifth av.

17 Broadway
100 Fourth av.
124 Irving pl.
200 Third av.
301 Second av.
400 First av.
500 Avenue A
— Avenue B

E. 20th, fr 133 Fifth av, E. to E. R.
1 Fifth av.
13 Broadway
101 Fourth av.
107 Gramercy pl.
128 Irving pl.
200 Third av.
300 Second av.
400 First av.
500 Avenue A
600 Avenue B

E. 21st, fr 147 Fifth av, E. to E. R.
2 Fifth av.
14 Broadway
100 Fourth av.
102 Gramercy pk.
121 Lexington av.
144 Gramercy pk.
200 Third av.
300 Second av.
400 First av.
500 Avenue A
— Avenue B
— Avenue C

E. 22d, fr 165 Fifth av, E. to E. R.
1 Fifth av.
5 Broadway
100 Fourth av.
132 Lexington av.
200 Third av.
300 Second av.
401 First av.
500 Avenue A
— Avenue B

E. 23d, fr 185 Fifth av, E. to E. R.
— Fifth av.
1 Broadway
— Madison av.
100 Fourth av.
135 Lexington av.
200 Third av.
300 Second av
400 First av.
500 Avenue A

E. 24th, fr 11 Madison av, E. to E. R.
1 Madison av.
100 Fourth av.
140 Lexington av.
200 Third av.
300 Second av.
401 First av.
500 Avenue A

E. 25th, fr 23 Madison av, E. to E. R.
1 Madison av.
23 Fourth av.
49 Lexington av.
81 Third av.
135 Second av.
183 First av.

E. 26th, fr 215 Fifth av, E. to E. R.
1 Fifth av.
27 Madison av.
100 Fourth av.
132 Lexington av.
153 Broadway al.
200 Third av.
300 Second av.
400 First av.

E. 27th, fr 231 Fifth av, E. to First av.
1 Fifth av.
23 Madison av.
100 Fourth av.
136 Lexington av.
— Broadway al.
200 Third av.
300 Second av.
— First av.

E. 28th, fr 249 Fifth av, E. to E. R.
1 Fifth av.
— Madison av.
100 Fourth av.
133 Lexington av.
200 Third av.
300 Second av.
400 First av.

E. 29th, fr 263 Fifth av, E. to E. R.
1 Fifth av.
26 Madison av.
100 Fourth av.
130 Lexington av.
200 Third av.
300 Second av.
406 First av.

E. 30th, fr 281 Fifth av, E. to E. R.
1 Fifth av.
— Madison av.
100 Fourth av.
132 Lexington av.
200 Third av.
302 Second av.
400 First av.

E. 31st, fr 299 Fifth av, E. to E. R.
1 Fifth av.
21 Madison av.
100 Fourth av.
132 Lexington av.
200 Third av.
300 Second av.
400 First av.

E. 32d, fr 315 Fifth av, E. to E. R.
1 Fifth av.
— Madison av.
100 Fourth av.
140 Lexington av.
203 Third av.
303 Second av.
400 First av.

E. 33d, fr 331 Fifth av, E. to E. R.
1 Fifth av.
29 Madison av.
100 Fourth av.
140 Lexington av.
200 Third av.
300 Second av.
400 First av.

E. 34th, fr 353 Fifth av, E. to E. R.
1 Fifth av.
28 Madison av.
101 Fourth av.
136 Lexington av.
200 Third av.
300 Second av.
401 First av.

E. 35th, fr 371 Fifth av, E. to E. R.
1 Fifth av.
— Madison av.
100 Fourth av.
138 Lexington av.
200 Third av.
300 Second av.
400 First av.

E. 36th, fr 387 Fifth av, E. to E. R.
1 Fifth av.
— Madison av.
33 Fourth av.
134 Lexington av.
162 Third av.
244 Second av.
— First av.

E. 37th, fr 409 Fifth av, E. to E. R.
1 Fifth av.
22 Madison av.
102 Fourth av.
125 Lexington av.
200 Third av.
300 Second av.
400 First av.

E. 38th, fr 421 Fifth av, E. to E. R.
1 Fifth av.
21 Madison av.
100 Fourth av.
127 Lexington av.
200 Third av.
300 Second av.
400 First av.

E. 39th, fr 439 Fifth av, E. to E. R.
1 Fifth av.
22 Madison av.
100 Fourth av.
130 Lexington av.
200 Third av.
300 Second av.
400 First av.

E. 40th, fr 461 Fifth av, E. to E. R.
2 Fifth av.
24 Madison av.
102 Fourth av.
132 Lexington av.
200 Third av.
300 Second av.
400 First av.

E. 41st, fr 477 Fifth av, E. to E. R.
1 Fifth av.
— Madison av.
101 Fourth av.
132 Lexington av.
200 Third av.
300 Second av.
400 First av.

E. 42d, fr 499 Fifth av, E. to E. R.
1 Fifth av.
24 Madison av.
— Fourth av.
— Lexington av.
125 Third av.
165 Second av.
— First av.

E. 43d, fr 519 Fifth av, E. to E. R.
1 Fifth av.
45 Madison av.
103 Fourth av.
— Lexington av.
200 Third av.
301 Second av.
400 First av.

E. 44th, fr Fifth av, E. to E. R.
1 Fifth av.
— Madison av.
— Fourth av.
— Lexington av.
— Third av.
— Second av.
— First av.

E. 45th, fr Fifth av, E. to E. R.
1 Fifth av.
— Madison av.
104 Fourth av.
124 Lexington av.
200 Third av.
305 Second av.
400 First av.

E. 46th, fr Fifth av, E. to E. R.
1 Fifth av.
— Madison av.
106 Fourth av.
— Lexington av.
200 Third av.
300 Second av.
401 First av.

E. 47th, fr Fifth av, E. to E. R.
1 Fifth av.
— Madison av.
— Fourth av.
— Lexington av.
— Third av.
163 Second av.
209 First av.

E. 48th, fr Fifth av, E. to E. R.
1 Fifth av.
— Madison av.
— Fourth av.
91 Lexington av.
121 Third av.
151 Second av.
206 First av.

E. 49th, fr Fifth av, E. to E. R.
1 Fifth av.
21 Madison av.
60 Fourth av.
— Lexington av.
121 Third av.
171 Second av.
257 First av.

E. 50th, fr Fifth av, E. to E. R.
1 Fifth av.
— Madison av.
— Fourth av.
— Lexington av.
136 Third av.
182 Second av.
246 First av.

E. 51st, fr Fifth av, E. to E. R.
1 Fifth av.
— Madison av.
105 Fourth av.
147 Lexington av.
200 Third av.
302 Second av.
412 First av.
— Avenue A

E. 52d, fr Fifth av, E. to E. R.
1 Fifth av.
41 Madison av.
108 Fourth av.
141 Lexington av.
200 Third av.
300 Second av.
— First av.

E. 53d, fr Fifth av, E. to E. R.
1 Fifth av.
48 Madison av.
101 Fourth av.
138 Lexington av.
200 Third av.
308 Second av.
402 First av.

E. 54th, fr Fifth av, E. to E. R.
1 Fifth av.
— Madison av.
— Fourth av.
128 Lexington av.
154 Third av.
— Second av.
352 First av.

E. 55th, fr Fifth av., E. to E. R.
— Fifth av.
— Madison av.
— Fourth av.
197 Lexington av.
249 Third av.
298 Second av.
— First av.

E. 58th, fr Fifth av, E. to E. R.
1 Fifth av.
— Fourth av.
— Lexington av
— Third av.
156 Second av.
195 First av.

E. 59th, fr Fifth av, E. to E. R.
1 Fifth av.
— Fourth av.
— Lexington av.
— Third av.
120 Second av.
— First av.

E. 60th, fr Fifth av, E. to E. R.
1 Fifth av.
— Fourth av.
84 Lexington av.
122 Third av.
— Second av.
— First av.

E. 82d, fr Fifth av, E. to E. R
— Fifth av.
— Madison av.
101 Fourth av.
200 Third av.
— Second av.

E. 84th, fr Fifth av, E. to E. R.
1 Fifth av.
— Fourth av.
134 Third av.
247 Second av.
226 First av.
— Avenue A

E. 86th, fr Fifth av, E. to E. R.
1 Fifth av.
100 Fourth av.
200 Third av.
300 Second av.
— First av.
— Avenue A

E. 117th, fr Fifth av, E. to Harlem River.
— Fifth av.
100 Fourth av.
200 Third av.

309 Second av.
411 First av.
510 Avenue A

E. 125th, fr Fifth av, E. to Harlem River
1 Fifth av.
68 Fourth av.
— Third av.
— Second av.

E. 128th, fr Fifth av, E. to Harlem River
1 Fifth av.
66 Fourth av.
174 Third av.
— Second av.

E. 129th, fr Fifth av. E. to Harlem River
1 Fifth av.
102 Fourth av.
201 Third av.
300 Second av.

E. Tompkins pl. 159 to 165 E. 11th

Edgar, fr 59 Greenwich, E. to Trinity pl.

Eighth, fr 94 Sixth av, E. to E. R.
Clinton pl. {
Sixth av.
Macdougal
Fifth av.
University pl.
Greene
Mercer }
129 Broadway
146 Lafayette pl.
— Astor pl.
151 Fourth av.
St. Mark's pl. {
Third av.
Second av.
First av.
Avenue A }
295 Avenue B
342 Avenue C
391 Avenue D
408 Lewis

Eighth av. fr Abingdon sq, N. to Harlem R.
1 Abingdon sq.
10 W. 12th
29 Jane
45 W. 4th
50 Horatio
63 W. 13th
68 Greenwich av.
78 W. 14th
98 W. 15th
122 W. 16th
141 W. 17th
159 W. 18th
175 W. 19th
193 W. 20th
210 W. 21st
230 W. 22d
250 W. 23d
271 W. 24th
288 W. 25th
306 W. 26th
324 W. 27th
342 W. 28th
360 W. 29th
378 W. 30th
394 W. 31st
414 W. 32d
434 W. 33d
450 W. 34th
468 W. 35th
489 W. 36th
505 W. 37th
536 W. 38th
539 W. 39th
556 W. 40th
576 W. 41st
594 W. 42d
610 W. 43d
625 W. 44th
646 W. 45th
657 W. 46th
673 W. 47th
689 W. 48th
707 W. 49th
721 W. 50th
739 W. 51st
746 W. 52d
753 W. 53d
771 W. 54th
789 W. 55th
803 W. 56th
820 W. 57th
838 W. 58th
855 W. 59th

Eldridge, fr 86 Division, N. to E. Houston
1 Division
27 Canal
56 Hester
88 Grand
108 Broome
132 Delancey
166 Rivington
194 Stanton
216 E. Houston

Eleventh av. fr 550 W. 14th, N. to W. 55th
1 W. 14th
22 W. 15th
42 W. 16th
62 W. 17th
82 W. 18th
102 W. 19th
122 W. 20th
142 W. 21st
162 W. 22d
182 W. 23d
202 W. 24th
222 W. 25th
242 W. 26th
262 W. 27th
282 W. 28th
302 W. 29th
318 W. 30th
337 W. 31st
358 W. 32d
377 W. 33d
398 W. 34th
418 W. 35th
438 W. 36th
456 W. 37th
476 W. 38th
496 W. 39th
514 W. 40th
534 W. 41st
552 W. 42d
572 W. 43d
590 W. 44th
610 W. 45th
628 W. 46th
646 W. 47th
666 W. 48th
684 W. 49th
702 W. 50th
722 W. 51st
738 W. 52d
743 Stryker's la.
758 W. 53d
778 W. 54th
796 W. 55th

Elizabeth, fr 52 Bayard, N. to Bleecker
1 Bayard
29 Canal
65 Hester
95 Grand
126 Broome
160 Spring
203 Prince
252 E. Houston
274 Bleecker

Elm, fr 12 Reade N. to Spring
1 Reade
2 Manhattan pl.
13 Duane
33 Pearl
45 Worth
56 Catharine la.
61 Leonard
74 Franklin
84 White
97 Walker
111 Canal
127 Howard
151 Grand
179 Broome
211 Marion
216 Spring

Essex, fr 162 Division, N. to E. Houston
1 Division
25 Hester
54 Grand
61 Essex m'k't pl.
76 Broome
96 Delancey
132 Rivington
157 Stanton
183 E. Houston

Essex m'k't, Essex c Grand

Essex m'k't pl. fr 68 Ludlow to Essex

Everett row, fr 64 W. 34th to Sixth av.

Exchange al. fr 55 Broadway, W. to Trinity pl.

Exchange pl fr 2 Hanover, W to Broadway

2 Hanover
28 William
59 Broad
70 New
— Broadway

Extra pl. r of 10 1st

Ferry, fr 84 Gold, S. E. to Pearl
1 Gold
19 Jacob
37 Cliff
59 Pearl

Fifth, fr 379 Bowery, E. to E. R.
1 Bowery
108 Second av.
205 First av.
303 Avenue A
401 Avenue B
503 Avenue C
605 Avenue D
632 Lewis

Fifth av. fr 57 Waverley pl, N. to Harlem R.
1 Washington sq N.
9 8th
23 9th
33 W. & E. 10th
43 W. 11th
60 W. & E. 12th
72 W. & E. 13th
84 W. & E. 14th
96 W. & E. 15th
108 W. & E. 16th
116 W. & E. 17th
128 W. & E. 18th
140 W. & E. 19th
154 W. & E. 20th
160 W. & E. 21st
170 W. & E. 22d
186 W. & E. 23d
196 Broadway
202 W. 25th
214 W. & E. 26th
232 W. & E. 27th
248 W. & E. 28th
264 W. & E. 29th
280 W. & E. 30th
299 W. & E. 31st
315 W. & E. 32d
331 W. & E. 33d
353 W. & E. 34th
370 W. & E. 35th
387 W. & E. 36th
409 W. & E. 37th
421 W. & E. 38th
439 W. & E. 39th
461 W. & E. 40th
477 E. 41st
499 W. & E. 42d
519 W. & E. 43d
Fr 43d to 129th not numbered.

First, fr 303 Bowery, E. to Avenue A
1 Bowery
10 Extra pl.
26 Second av.
72 First av.
124 Avenue A

First av. (Allen st.), fr 164 E. Houston, N. to Harlem R.
1 E. Houston
11 1st
31 2d
49 3d
59 E. 4th
75 5th
95 6th
107 7th
125 St. Mark's pl.
135 9th
151 E. 10th
167 E. 11th
185 E. 12th
207 E. 13th
223 E. 14th
243 E. 15th
265 E. 16th
281 E. 17th
297 E. 18th
313 E. 19th
329 E. 20th
347 E. 21st
363 E. 22d
382 E. 23d
401 E. 24th
418 E. 25th
433 E. 26th
449 E. 27th
465 E. 28th
481 E. 29th
497 E. 30th
525 E. 31st
543 E. 32d
567 E. 33d
583 E. 34th
599 E. 35th

Fitzroy pl. 357 W. 28th

Fletcher, fr 820 Pearl, S. to East River
1 Pearl
15 Water
28 Front
45 South

Forsyth, fr 68 Division, N. to E. Houston
1 Division
2 Bayard
29 Canal
61 Hester
92 Grand
108 Broome
132 Delancey
166 Rivington
191 Stanton
219 E. Houston

Fourth av. fr 402 Bowery, N. Harlem
2 Bowery
— 6th
— 7th
34 Astor pl.
38 8th
57 9th
73 E. 10th
91 E. 11th
109 E. 12th
129 E. 13th
151 E. 14th
Union sq. { E. 15th, E. 16th, E. 17th, E. 18th, E. 19th }
250 E. 20th
266 E. 21st
284 E. 22d
295 E. 23d
315 E. 24th
333 E. 25th
353 E. 26th
373 E. 27th
386 E. 28th
402 E. 29th
418 E. 30th
438 E. 31st
458 E. 32d
Park av. { E. 33d, E. 34th, E. 35th, E. 36th, E. 37th, E. 38th, E. 39th }
617 E. 40th
635 E. 41st
651 E. 42d

Frankfort, fr 166 Nassau, E. to Pearl
1 Nassau
2 Chatham
17 William
16 N. William
36 Rose
47 Gold
54 Vandewater
65 Jacob
76 Cliff
92 Pearl

Franklin, fr 64 Baxter, W. to N. R.
1 Baxter
20 Centre
38 Elm
56 Cortlandt al.
64 Broadway
68 Franklin pl.
94 Church
124 W. Broadway
130 Varick
165 Hudson
194 Greenwich
200 Washington
219 West

Franklin M'k't, Old slip

Franklin al. fr 70 Franklin, N. to White

Franklin sq. fr Cherry to Pearl

Franklin ter. r 364 W. 26th

Front, fr 49 Whitehall, E. to Roosevelt, and fr

Montgomery c South, E. to E. R.
1 Whitehall
5 Moore
21 Broad
39 Coenties' sl.
53 Cuyler's al.
75 Old sl.
93 Gouverneur's la.
101 Jones' la.
113 Wall
131 Pine
137 Depeyster
151 Maiden la.
159 Fletcher
175 Burling sl.
199 Fulton
209 Beekman
235 Peck sl.
259 Dover
273 Roosevelt
289 Montgomery
305 Gouverneur sl.
344 Jackson
— Corlears

Fulton, fr 93 South, W. to N. R.
1 South
18 Front
25 Water
37 Pearl
53 Cliff
68 Ryder's al.
79 Gold
101 William
110 Dutch
125 Nassau
157 Broadway
189 Church
225 Greenwich
237 Washington
260 West

Fulton m'kt, Fulton c South

Gansevoort, fr 355 W. Fourth, W. to N. R.
1 W. 13th
2 W. 4th
19 Hudson
— W. 12th
36 Greenwich
— Ninth av.
51 Washington
78 West
— Thirteenth av.

Garden row, r 138 W. 11th

Gay, fr 141 Waverley pl, N. to Christopher

Gilford pl. E. 45th, fr Lexington to Third av.

Glover pl. Thompson street bet Spring and Prince

Goerck, fr 574 Grand, N. to E. R.
1 Grand
2 Rachel la.
19 Broome
49 Delancey
79 Rivington
117 Stanton
143 E. Houston
159 Third

Gold, fr 87 Maiden la, N. to Frankfort
1 Maiden la.
15 Platt
23 John
36 Ryder's al.
51 Fulton
59 Ann
65 Beekman
77 Spruce
84 Ferry
103 Frankfort

Gouverneur, fr 275 Division, S. to Water
1 Division
5 E. Broadway
20 Henry
33 Madison
51 Monroe
63 Cherry
71 Water

Gouverneur la. fr 48 South to Water
1 South
14 Front
— Water

Gouverneur m'k't. See Gouverneur sl.

Gouverneur sl. fr 371 South, N. to Water
1 South
2 Front
12 Water

Gramercy pk. bet Third and Fourth, and E. 20th and E. 21st sts.

Gramercy pl. E. 20th, fr 100 to 146

Grand, fr 80 Varick, E. to E. R.
1 Varick
17 Sullivan
33 Thompson
51 Laurens
69 Wooster
87 Greene
104 Mercer
114 Broadway
131 Crosby
151 Elm
163 Centre
172 Centre m'k't pl.
173 Baxter
189 Mulberry
205 Mott
219 Elizabeth
235 Bowery
253 Chrystie
269 Forsyth
289 Eldridge
307 Allen
321 Orchard
339 Ludlow
355 Essex
373 Norfolk
389 Suffolk
407 Clinton
423 Attorney
441 Ridge
459 Pitt
471 Division
484 Willett
502 Sheriff
503 E. Broadway
520 Columbia
527 Henry
540 Cannon
541 Jackson
556 Lewis
567 Madison
574 Goerck
587 Corlears
590 Mangin
599 Monroe
606 Tompkins
622 East

Great Jones, fr 682 Broadway, E. to Bowery
1 Broadway
8 Lafayette pl.
58 Bowery

Greene, fr 331 Canal, N. to Clinton pl.
1 Canal
35 Grand
55 Broome
85 Spring
117 Prince
149 W. Houston
182 Bleecker
192½ Amity la.
214 Amity
229 W. Fourth
247 Washington pl.
251 Waverley pl.
260 Clinton pl.

Greenwich, fr 4 Battery pl, N. to Gansevoort
1 Battery pl.
39 Morris
59 Edgar
89 Rector
112 Carlisle
122 Albany
131 Thames
139 Cedar
147 Liberty
169 Cortlandt
185 Dey
197 Fulton
213 Vesey
229 Barclay
249 Robinson
267 Murray
283 Warren
291 Chambers

511 Reade
523 Duane
337 Jay
353 Harrison
369 Franklin
383 North Moore
397 Beach
413 Hubert
427 Laight
441 Vestry
455 Desbrosses
469 Watts
477 Canal
513 Spring
531 Vandam
549 Charlton
565 King
589 W. Houston
599 Clarkson
615 Leroy
629 Morton
641 Barrow
677 Christopher
695 W. Tenth
711 Charles
731 Perry
751 W. 11th
769 Bank
782 Bethune
795 W. 12th
807 Jane
819 Horatio
834 Gansevoort

Greenwich av. fr 105 Sixth av, N. to Eighth av.
1 Sixth av.
5 Christopher
14 W. 10th
37 Charles
55 Perry
71 W. 11th
72 Seventh av
85 Bank
88 W. 12th
113 Jane
120 W. 13th
129 Horatio
136 Eighth av.

Grove, fr 488 Hudson, E. to Waverley pl.
1 Hudson
15 Bedford
45 Bleecker
77 W. 4th
80 W. Wash'n pl.
98 Waverley pl.

Hague, fr 367 Pearl, W. to Cliff

Hall pl. fr 2 6th, N. to 7th

Hamersley pl. W. Houston, bet Macdougal and Congress

Hamilton, fr 73 Catharine, E. to market

Hamilton pl. W. 51st, bet B'way and Eighth av.

Hancock (Cottage pl.) fr 176 W. Houston, N. to Bleecker

Hanover, fr 59 Wall, S. to Pearl
1 Wall
2 Exchange pl.
5 Beaver
9 Pearl

Hanover sq. Pearl st, fr 105 Pearl to Stone

Harrison, fr 81 Hudson, W. to N. R.
1 Hudson
5 Staple
23 Greenwich
33 Washington
55 West

Harwood pl. E. 78th, bet Third and Fourth avs.

Henry, fr 16 Oliver, E. to Grand
1 Oliver
13 Catharine
64 Market
84 Birmingham
101 Pike
144 Rutgers
174 Jefferson
206 Clinton
247 Montgomery
268 Gouverneur
284 Scammel
325 Grand
338 Jackson

Herman pl. r 220 E. 4th

Hester, fr 216½ Division, W. to Centre
1 Clinton
2 Division
15 Suffolk
31 Norfolk
47 Essex
63 Ludlow
79 Orchard
93 Allen
105 Eldridge
119 Forsyth
135 Chrystie
151 Bowery
159 Elizabeth
175 Mott
191 Mulberry
207 Baxter
219 Centre

Hester ct. r 103 Hester

Hoboken, fr 474 Washington, W. to N. R.

Horatio, fr 129 Greenwich av. W. to N. R.
2 Greenwich av.
1 Eighth av.
5 W. 4th
41 Hudson
59 Greenwich
87 Washington
117 West
— Thirteenth av.

Howard, fr 201 Centre, W. to Mercer
1 Centre
9 Elm
28 Crosby
41 Broadway
53 Mercer

Hubert, fr 149 Hudson, W. to N. R.
1 Hudson
9 Collister
19 Greenwich
33 Washington
50 West

Hudson, fr 139 Chambers, N. to Ninth av.
1 Chambers
5 Reade
29 Duane
50 Thomas
61 Jay
72 Worth
81 Harrison
92 Leonard
100 Franklin
119 N. Moore
133 Beach
149 Hubert
163 Laight
179 Vestry
195 Desbrosses
211 Canal
214 Watts
230 Broome
262 Dominick
298 Spring
322 Vandam
344 Charlton
364 King
384 W. Houston
402 Clarkson
421 Leroy
436 Morton
462 Barrow
488 Grove
499 Christopher
515 W. 10th
533 Charles
549 Perry
567 W. 11th
585 Bank
609 W. 12th
621 Jane
635 Horatio
649 Gansevoort
662 W. 13th
686 W. 14th
692 Ninth av.

Hudson pl. W. 34th, bet Ninth & Tenth avs.

Irving pl. fr E. 14th, N. to E. 20th
1 E. 14th
14 E. 15th
32 E. 16th
50 E. 17th
64 E. 18th
78 E. 19th
86 E. 20th

Jackson, fr 338 Henry, S. to E. R.
1 Henry
2 Grand
13 Madison
26 Monroe
44 Cherry
62 Water
78 Front
88 South

Jackson pl. r 16 Downing

Jacob, fr 19 Ferry, N. to Frankfort

James, fr 175 Chatham, S. to James sl.
1 Chatham
11 New Bowery
37 Madison
71 Oak
85 Batavia
101 New Chambers
104 Cherry

James sl. fr 77 Cherry, S. to E. R.
1 Cherry
8 Water
20 South

Jane, fr 113 Greenwich av, W. to N. R.
1 Greenwich av.
31 W. 4th
33 Eighth av.
58 Hudson
65 Greenwich
95 Washington
— West
— Thirteenth av.

Jauncey ct. 37 to 43 Wall

Jay, fr 61 Hudson, W. to N. R.
1 Hudson
7 Staple
18 Greenwich
25 Washington
34 Caroline
49 West

Jefferson, fr 179 Division, S. to E. R.
1 Division
4 E. Broadway
22 Henry
26½ Madison
30 Monroe
36 Cherry
— Water
— South

Jefferson m'k't, Greenwich av c Sixth av.

Jersey, fr 127 Crosby, E. to Mulberry

John, fr 191 Broadway, E. to Pearl
1 Broadway
31 Nassau
49 Dutch
65 William
87 Gold
101 Cliff
119 Pearl

Jones, fr 176 W. 4th, W. to Bleecker

Jones' la. fr 101 Front, S. to E. R.

Johnson's row, W. 15th, fr 477 to 495

King, fr 41 Macdougal, W. to N. R.
1 Macdougal
13 Congress
57 Varick
91 Hudson
119 Greenwich
133 Washington
138 West

Knapp's pl. r 422 E. 10th

Lafayette pl. fr 8 Gt. Jones, N. to 8th
1 Gt. Jones
12 E. 4th
63 Astor pl.
— 8th

Laight, fr 398 Canal, W. to N. R.
1 Canal
11 St. John's la.
22 Varick
48 Hudson
55 Collister
66 Greenwich
76 Washington
90 West

Lamartine pl. W. 29th, bet Eighth & Ninth avs.

Laurens, fr 375 Canal, N. to Amity
1 Canal
28 Grand
55 Broome
91 Spring
124 Prince
162 W. Houston
— Amity

Lawrence, fr W. 126th, n Ninth av, to W. 129th
1 W. 126th
— W. 127th
— Tenth av.
— W. 128th
— W. 129th

Leandert's pl. fr 183 7th

Lennox pl. W. 22d, bet Eighth & Ninth avs.

Leonard, fr 90 Hudson, E. to Baxter
1 Hudson
35 W. Broadway
63 Church
96 Broadway
109 Benson
120 Elm
141 Centre
163 Baxter

Leroy, fr 238 Bleecker, W. to N. R.
1 Bleecker
31 Bedford
98 Hudson
123 Greenwich
143 Washington
162 West

Leroy pl Bleecker, bet Mercer & Greene

Lewis, fr 556 Grand, N. to 8th
1 Grand
19 Broome
44 Delancey
72 Rivington
99 Stanton
127 E. Houston
149 3d
169 E. 4th
183 5th
199 6th
217 7th
231 8th

Lexington av. fr 191 E. 21st, N. to E. 63d
1 E. 21st
8 E. 22d
16 E. 23d
28 E. 24th
50 E. 25th
68 E. 26th
88 E. 27th
105 E. 28th
123 E. 29th
145 E. 30th
163 E. 31st
170 E. 32d
191 E. 33d
211 E. 34th
227 E. 35th

236 E. 36th
264 E. 37th
275 E. 38th
303 E. 39th
324 E. 40th
344 E. 41st

Liberty, fr 76 Maiden la, W. to N. R.
1 Maiden la.
13 William
51 Nassau
57 Liberty pl.
75 Broadway
88 Temple
98 Trinity pl.
123 Greenwich
137 Washington
147 West

Liberty ct. 4 & 6 Liberty pl.

Liberty pl. fr 57 Liberty, N. to Maiden la.

Lispenard, fr 151 W. B'way, E. to Broadway
1 W. Broadway
3 Church
71 Broadway

Liv'gston pl. fr 325 E. 15th, N. to E. 17th
1 E. 15th
9 E. 16th
16 E. 17th

London ter. W. 23d, bet Ninth & Tenth avs.

Lord's ct. r 51 Beaver

Ludlow, fr 144 Division, N. to E. Houston
1 Division
2 Canal
31 Hester
59 Grand
68 Essex m'k't pl.
79 Broome
101 Delancey
127 Rivington
159 Stanton
192 E. Houston

Ludlow pl. W. Houston, bet Sullivan & Macdougal

Macdougal, fr 219 Spring, N. to Clinton pl
1 Spring
7 Miller's pl.
13 Vandam
29 Charlton
34 Prince
41 King
59 W. Houston
89 Bleecker
113 Minetta la.
131 Amity
141 W. 4th
155 W. Wash'n pl.
165 Waverley pl.
181 Clinton pl.

Madison, fr 426 Pearl, E. to Grand
1 Pearl
- New Chambers
6 Chestnut
9 Roosevelt
20 New Bowery
40 James
56 Oliver
67 Catharine
122 Market
137 Birmingham
156 Pike
199 Rutgers
224 Jefferson
258 Clinton
297 Montgomery
316 Gouverneur
328 Scammel
385 Jackson
411 Grand

Madison av. from E. 23d, N. to Harlem R.
1 E. 23d
11 E. 24th
23 E. 25th
33 E. 26th
53 E. 27th
69 E. 28th
85 E. 29th
103 E. 30th
118 E. 31st
134 E. 32d
149 E. 33d
165 E. 34th
179 E. 35th
193 E. 36th
210 E. 37th
222 E. 38th
239 E. 39th
258 E. 40th
274 E. 41st
— E. 42d

Madison ct. r 237 Madison

Madison sq. N., E. 26th, bet Fifth & Madison avs.

Maiden la. fr 127 B'way, S.E. to E. R.
1 Broadway
18 Liberty pl.
27 Nassau
65 William
76 Liberty
87 Gold
114 Pearl
134 Water
144 Front
168 South

Mangin, fr 590 Grand, N. to E. R.
1 Grand
3 Rachel la.
16 Broome
43 Delancey
61 Manhattan pl.
77 Rivington
97 Stanton
145 E. Houston

Manhattan, fr 444 E. Houston, N. to 3d

Manhattan, fr W. 125th, n Ninth av, to Twelfth av.
1 W. 125th
- W. 126th
- Tenth av.
- W. 127th
— W. 128th
— Eleventh av.

Manhat'n pl. r 63 to 71 Mangin

Manhat'n pl. fr 6 Elm, W. & S. to Reade

Mansfield pl. W. 51st, bet Eighth & Ninth avs.

Marion, fr 404 Broome, N.
1 Broome
35 Spring
72 Prince
86 ———

Market, fr 61 Division, S. to E. R.
1 Division
7 E. Broadway
22 Henry
40 Madison
56 Monroe
58 Hamilton
77 Cherry
93 Water
101 South

Marketfield, fr 1 Whitehall, E. to Broad

Martin ter. E. 30th, bet Second & Third avs.

Mechanic al. fr 72 Monroe to Cherry

Mechanic pl. r 26 Avenue A

Mercer, fr 318 Canal, N. to Clinton pl.
1 Canal
14 Howard
32 Grand
49 Broome
77 Spring
115 Prince
150 W. Houston

177 Bleecker
217 Amity
233 W. 4th
246 Washington pl.
— Waverley pl.
260 Clinton pl.

Mill la. fr 61 Stone, N. W. to S. William

Miller's pl. r 4 Macdougal

Milligan pl. r 139 Sixth av.

Millward pl. W. 31st, bet Eighth & Ninth avs.

Minetta, fr 205 Bleecker, N. to Minetta la.
1 Bleecker
2 Minetta pl.
19 Minetta la.

Minetta la. fr 113 Macdougal, W. to Sixth av.
1 Macdougal
5 Minetta
27 Sixth av.

Minetta pl. r 2 Minetta

Mission pl. fr 60 Park, N. to Worth

Monroe, fr 59 Catharine, E. to Grand
1 Catharine
45 Market
72 Mechanic al.
77 Pike
98 Pelham
119 Rutgers
146 Jefferson
148 Clinton
182 Montgomery
208 Gouverneur
220 Scammel
273 Jackson
312 Corlears
334 Grand

Monroe pl. Monroe st, fr 207 to 213

Montgomery fr 247 Division, S. to E. R.
1 Division
5 E. Broadway
15 Henry
33 Madison
55 Monroe
71 Cherry
79 Water
87 Front
95 South

Moore, fr 30 Pearl, S. to E. R.
1 Pearl
5 Water
18 Front
36 South

Morris, fr 25 Broadway, W. to N. R.
1 Broadway
11 Greenwich
15 Washington
27 West

Morris pl. W. 42d, bet Tenth & Eleventh avs.

Morton, fr 256 Bleecker, W. to N. R.
1 Bleecker
29 Bedford
66 Hudson
89 Greenwich
97 Washington
114 West

Mott, from 180 Chatham, N. to Bleecker
1 Chatham
21 Park
38 Pell
50 Bayard
82 Canal
114 Hester
149 Grand
173 Broome
206 Spring
240 Prince
288 E. Houston
321 Bleecker

Mulberry, fr 156 Chatham, N. to Bleecker
1 Chatham
29 Park
71 Bayard
96 Canal
128 Hester
152 Grand
176 Broome
211 Spring
256 Prince
271 Jersey
293 E. Houston
308 Bleecker

Murray, fr 247 Broadway, W. to N. R.
1 Broadway
29 Church
61 College pl.
87 Greenwich
95 Washington
111 West

Nassau, fr 20 Wall, N. to Chatham
1 Wall
11 Pine
25 Cedar
39 Liberty
55 Maiden la.
69 John
91 Fulton
105 Ann
137 Beekman
151 Spruce
166 Frankfort

Neilson pl. Mercer, bet Waverley pl & 8th st.

New, fr 7 Wall, S. to Beaver
1 Wall
29 Exchange pl.
81 Beaver

New Bowery, fr 394 Pearl, N. to Chatham
2 Pearl
1 Oak
3 Chestnut
9 New Chambers
17 Roosevelt
26 Madison
41 James
63 Oliver

New Chambers, fr 67 Chatham, E. to Cherry
1 Chatham
2 Duane
9 William
36 Rose
42 Pearl
— Madison
49 Chestnut
50 New Bowery
55 Roosevelt
60 Oak
70 Batavia
94 Cherry
89 James

Ninth, fr 112 Sixth av, E. to E. R.
1 Sixth av.
66 Fifth av.
99 University pl.
138 Broadway
154 Fourth av.
168 Third av.
176 Stuyvesant
207 Second av.
251 First av.
296 Avenue A
300 Avenue B
348 Avenue C
399 Avenue D

Ninth av. fr Gansevoort, N. to Harlem R.
1 Gansevoort
4 W. 12th
18 W. 13th
31 W. 14th
52 Hudson
59 W. 15th
75 W. 16th
92 W. 17th
108 W. 18th
121 W. 19th
140 W. 20th
154 W. 21st
171 W. 22d
182 W. 23d
205 W. 24th
220 W. 25th

242 W. 26th
258 W. 27th
279 W. 28th
294 W. 29th
312 W. 30th
332 W. 31st
357 W. 32d
368 W. 33d
389 W. 34th
407 W. 35th
413 W. 36th
426 W. 37th
442 W. 38th
473 W. 39th
474 W. 40th
492 W. 41st
512 W. 42d
541 W. 43d
550 W. 44th
562 W. 45th
585 W. 46th
598 W. 47th
612 W. 48th
628 W. 49th
649 W. 50th
661 W. 51st
676 W. 52d
694 W. 53d
713 W. 54th
727 W. 55th

Norfolk, fr 180 Division, N. to E. Houston
1 Division
14 Hester
38 Grand
59 Broome
80 Delancey
116 Rivington
135 Stanton
167 E. Houston

N. Moore, fr 122 W. Broadway, W. to N. R.
1 West B'way
17 Varick
47 Hudson
73 Greenwich
85 Washington
107 West

N. William, fr 16 Frankfort, N. to Chatham
1 Frankfort
4 William
31 Chatham

Nyack pl. r 149 Bank

Oak, fr 392 Pearl, E. to Catharine
1 Pearl
2 New Bowery
8 Chestnut
16 New Chambers
17 Roosevelt
37 James
49 Oliver
59 Catharine

Old sl. fr 66 Stone, S. to E. R.
1 Stone
2 Pearl
15 Water
25 Front
33 South

Oliver, fr 63 New Bowery, S. to E. R.
1 NewBowery
16 Henry
32 Madison
58 Oak
84 Cherry
94 Water
102 South

Orchard, fr 124 Division, N. to E. Houston
1 Division
9 Canal
38 Hester
64 Grand
88 Broome
115 Delancey
143 Rivington
171 Stanton
201 E. Houston

Pacific pl. r 133 W. 29th

Pagoda pl. foot E. 120th

Park, fr 36 Centre, E. to Mott
27 Centre
45 Pearl
60 Mission pl.
81 Baxter
98 Mulberry
— Mott

Park av. Fourth av, fr E. 34th to E. 39th
1 E. 34th
17 E. 35th
37 E. 36th
56 E. 37th
65 E. 38th
— E. 39th

Park pl. fr 237 Broadway, W. to College pl.
1 Broadway
28 Church
58 College pl.

Park row, fr 1 Ann, E. to Spruce
1 Ann
34 Beekman
41 Spruce

Patchin pl. r 111 W. 10th

Pearl, fr 13 State, E. & N. to B'way
1 State
23 Whitehall
30 Moore
53 Broad
66 Coenties sl.
73 Coenties al.
106 Hanover sq.
110 Old sl.
105 William
121 Hanover
141 Beaver
152 Wall
168 Pine
181 Cedar
194 Maiden la.
208 Fletcher
221 Platt
234 Burling sl.
235 John
265 Fulton
285 Beekman
309 Ferry
312 Peck sl.
340 Dover
342 Franklin sq.
351 Frankfort
367 Hague
392 Oak
394 New Bowery
399 Vandewater
414 New Chambers
421 Rose
426 Madison
447½ Williams
464 Chatham
485 City Hall pl.
502 Park
512 Centre
536 Elm
557 Broadway

Peck sl. fr 31 Pearl, E. to South
1 Pearl
16 Water
28 Front
42 South

Pelham, fr 98 Monroe, E. to Cherry

Pell, fr 18 Bowery, W. to Mott
1 Bowery
15 Doyers
36 Mott

Perry, fr 55 Greenwich av, W. to N. R.
1 Greenwich av.
15 Waverley pl.
47 W. 4th
79 Bleecker
95 Hudson
108 Greenwich
138 Washington
165 West

Phelps pl. E 30th, bet First & Second avs.

Pike, fr 107 Division, S. to E R.
1 Division
7 E. Broadway
21 Henry
37 Madison
57 Monroe
69 Cherry
77 Water
90 South

Pine, fr 106 Broadway, E. to E. R.
1 Broadway
20 Nassau

46 William
77½ Pearl
84 Water
89 Front
100 South

Pitt, fr 276 Division, N. to E. Houston
1 Division
2 Grand
21 Broome
41 Delancey
79 Rivington
111 Stanton
142 E. Houston

Platt, fr 221 Pearl, W. to William
1 Pearl
20 Gold
41 William

Prince, fr 240 Bowery, W. to Macdougal
1 Bowery
15 Elizabeth
33 Mott
46 Mulberry
60 Marion
70 Crosby
79 Broadway
91 Mercer
107 Greene
125 Wooster
145 Laurens
165 Thompson
185 Sullivan
205 Macdougal

Rachel la. fr 2 Goerck, E. to Mangin

Randall pl. 9th st, bet B'way & University pl.

Reade, fr 73 Duane, W. to N. R.
- Duane
- City Hall pl.
1 Centre
12 Elm
34 Manhattan pl.
— Broadway
80 Church
112 W. Broadway
127 Hudson
160 Greenwich
174 Washington
197 West

Rector, fr 73 Broadway, W. to N. R.
1 Broadway
3 Trinity pl.
11 Greenwich
23 Washington
35 West

Renwick, fr 486 Canal, N. to Spring

Ridge, fr 254 Division, N. to E. Houston
1 Division
5 Grand
27 Broome
45 Delancey
78 Rivington
104 Stanton
130 E. Houston

Rivington, fr 213 Bowery, E. to E. R.
1 Bowery
17 Chrystie
35 Forsyth
49 Eldridge
67 Allen
83 Orchard
97 Ludlow
115 Essex
129 Norfolk
145 Suffolk
163 Clinton
179 Attorney
193 Ridge
215 Pitt
231 Willett
251 Sheriff
267 Columbia
287 Cannon
305 Lewis
316 Rivington pl.
321 Goerck
337 Mangin
355 Tompkins
375 East

Rivingt'n pl. r 316 Rivington

Robinson, fr 4 College pl, W. to N. R.
38 College pl.
49 Greenwich
60 Washington
80 West

Roosevelt, fr 147 Chatham, S. to E. R.
1 Chatham
37 Madison
40 New Bowery
59 New Chambers
71 Oak
78 Batavia
101 Cherry
117 Water
131 Front
— South

Rose, fr 36 Frankfort, N.E. to Pearl
1 Frankfort
40 Duane
6? New Chambers
65 Pearl

Roslyn pl. Greene st, bet Amity & W. 4th

Russell pl. Greenwich av, bet Charles and Perry

Rutgers, fr 24 Canal, S. to E. R.
2 Canal
1 E. Broadway
13 Henry
31 Madison
45 Monroe
59 Cherry
68 Water
80 South

Rutgers pl. Monroe, fr Jefferson to Clinton

Rutherford pl. fr 224 E. 17th to E. 15th
1 E. 17th
8 E. 16th
- E. 15th

Ryder's al. fr 68 Fulton to Gold

St. Clement's pl. Macdougal, fr W. Houston to Bleecker & fr Waverley pl to Clinton pl.

St. George's pl. E. 13th bet Second & First avs.

St. John's la. fr 6 Beach, N. to Laight
1 Beach
9 York
16 Laight

St. Luke's pl. Leroy st, fr 63 to 99

St. Mark's pl. 8th st, fr Third av, E. to Avenue A
1 Third av.
38 Second av.
82 First av.
127 Avenue A

St. Nicholas av. fr cor Sixth av. & W. 110th to Ninth av. & W. 145th, & fr there to W. 155th & Kingsbridge road

St. Timothy's pl. W. 52d, bet B'way & Eighth av.

Scammel, fr 299 E. B'way, S. to Water
1 E. B'way
7 Henry
26 Madison
38 Monroe

49 Cherry
58 Water

Second, fr 321 Bowery, E. to Avenue D
1 Bowery
35 Second av.
87 First av.
145 Avenue A
201 Avenue B
258 Avenue C
297 Sheriff
314 Avenue D

Second av. fr 118 E. Houston, N. to Harlem R.
1 E. Houston
17 1st
35 2d
53 3d
67 E. 4th
85 5th
100 6th
114 7th
128 St. Mark's pl.
140 9th
154 E. 10th
155 Stuyvesant
174 E. 11th
190 E. 12th
203 E. 13th
219 E. 14th
— E. 15th
— E. 17th
311 E. 18th
327 E. 19th
342 E. 20th
361 E. 21st
379 E. 22d
398 E. 23d
416 E. 24th
438 E. 25th
458 E. 26th
476 E. 27th
498 E. 28th
524 E. 29th
540 E. 30th
562 E. 31st
578 E. 32d
598 E. 33d
620 E. 34th
638 E. 35th
660 E. 36th
688 E. 37th
700 E. 38th
724 E. 39th
476 E. 40th
765 E. 41st
777 E. 42d
799 E. 43d
822 E. 44th
838 E. 45th
857 E. 46th
877 E. 47th
899 E. 48th
923 E. 49th
941 E. 50th
961 E. 51st
982 E. 52d
1003 E. 53d
1031 E. 54th
1044 E. 55th
1062 E. 56th
1082 E. 57th
1102 E. 58th
1122 E. 59th
1138 E. 60th

Seventh, fr Fourth av, E. to E. R.
1 Fourth av.
— Third av.
— Hall pl.
48 Second av.
87 First av.
130 Avenue A
200 Avenue B
183 Leandert's pl.
229 Avenue C
282 Avenue D
300 Lewis

Seventh av. fr 72 Greenwich av, N. to Harlem R.
2 Greenwich av.
1 W. 11th
10 W. 12th
32 W. 13th
47 W. 14th
58 W. 15th
79 W. 16th
95 W. 17th
109 W. 18th
126 W. 19th
141 W. 20th
157 W. 21st
178 W. 22d
185 W. 23d
209 W. 24th
225 W. 25th
244 W. 26th
262 W. 27th
279 W. 28th
295 W. 29th
312 W. 30th
332 W. 31st
347 W. 32d
363 W. 33d
382 W. 34th
401 W. 35th
419 W. 36th
439 W. 37th
459 W. 38th
460 W. 39th
487 W. 40th
504 W. 41st
521 W. 42d
537 W. 43d
— W. 44th
— Broadway
— W. 45th
607 W. 46th
635 W. 47th
649 W. 48th
667 W. 49th

Sheriff, fr 502 Grand, N. to 2d
1 Grand
20 Broome
44 Delancey
71 Rivington
99 Stanton
127 E. Houston
— Second

Sixth, fr 395 Bowery, E. to E. R.
1 Bowery
2 Hall pl.
30 Second av.
68 First av.
114 Avenue A
160 Avenue B
171 Sixth st. ct.
206 Avenue C
258 Avenue D
274 Lewis

Sixth st. ct. r 169 Sixth

Sixth av. fr 1 Carmine, N. to Harlem R.
1 Carmine
2 Minetta la.
16 Amity
37 W. 4th
56 W. Wash'n pl.
74 Waverley pl.
94 Eighth
105 Gr'nwich av.
112 Ninth
131 W. 10th
139 Milligan pl
146 W. 11th
168 W. 12th
187 W. 13th
207 W. 14th
227 W. 15th
248 W. 16th
266 W. 17th
286 W. 18th
302 W. 19th
319 W. 20th
337 W. 21st
355 W. 22d
373 W. 23d
391 W. 24th
409 W. 25th
427 W. 26th
444 W. 27th
461 W. 28th
476 W. 29th
495 W. 30th
520 W. 31st
531 W. 32d
551 W. 33d
569 Broadway
571 W. 34th
594 W. 35th
612 W. 36th
632 W. 37th
654 W. 38th
677 W. 39th
697 W. 40th
717 W. 41st
737 W. 42d
757 W. 43d
777 W. 44th
797 W. 45th
812 W. 46th
832 W. 47th
850 W. 48th
870 W. 49th
886 W. 50th
— W. 51st
928 W. 52d
950 W. 53d
970 W. 54th
988 W. 55th
1010 W. 56th
1030 W. 57th
1050 W. 58th
1070 W. 59th

South, fr 54 Whitehall, E. to E. R.
1 Whitehall
7 Moore
14 Broad

22 Coenties sl.
28 Cuyler's al.
39 Old sl.
48 Gouverneur la.
52 Jones' la.
59 Wall
68 Pine
70 Depeyster
75 Maiden la.
77 Fletcher
87 Burling sl.
93 Fulton
104 Beekman
118 Peck sl.
160 Dover
175 Roosevelt
187 James sl.
194 Oliver
202 Catharine sl.
221 Market
240 Pike
262 Rutgers
269 Jefferson
285 Clinton
363 Montgomery
371 Gouverneur sl.
381 Jackson
— Corlears

S. William, fr 7 William, W. to Broad
1 William
2 Beaver
7 Mill la.
43 Broad

Spingler pl. E. 15th, fr 5th av to Broadway

Spring, fr 188½ Bowery, W. to N. R.
1 Bowery
11 Elizabeth
27 Mott
45 Mulberry
61 Marion
64 Elm
77 Crosby
89 B'way
101 Mercer
121 Greene
141 Wooster
157 Laurens
177 Thompson
197 Sullivan
219 Macdougal
226 Clarke
259 Varick
291 Hudson
306 Renwick
317 Greenwich
333 Washington
353 West

Spruce, fr 41 Park row, S. E. to Gold
1 Park row
2 Nassau
23 William
43 Gold

Stanton, fr 245 Bowery, E. to E. R.
1 Bowery
8 Stanton pl.
25 Chrystie
39 Forsyth
58 Eldridge
72 Allen
88 Orchard
103 Ludlow
117 Essex
136 Norfolk
149 Suffolk
166 Clinton
186 Attorney
200 Ridge
219 Pitt
239 Willett
255 Sheriff
270 Columbia
284 Cannon
297 Lewis
319 Goerck
339 Mangin
— Tompkins

Stanton pl. r 8 Stanton

Staple, fr 169 Duane, N. to Harrison
1 Duane
2 Jay
6 Harrison

State, fr 48 Whitehall to Broadway
1 Whitehall
13 Pearl
15 Bridge
20 Bowling gr.

Stone, fr 13 Whitehall, E. to William
1 Whitehall
19 Broad
40 Coenties al.
61 Mill la.
67 William

Stryker's la. r 743 Eleventh av.

Stryker's row, W. 52d bet Tenth and Eleventh avs.

Stuyvesant, fr 25 Third av, E. to Second av.
1 Third av.
13 9th
37 10th
— Second av.

Suffolk, fr 202 Division, N. to E. Houston
1 Divison
6 Hester
37 Grand
61 Broome
92 Delancey
102 Clinton al.
120 Rivington
149 Stanton
188 E. Houston

Sullivan, fr 415 Canal, N. to Amity
1 Canal
21 Grand
46 Watts
55 Broome
91 Spring
129 Prince
162 W. Houston
204 Bleecker
236 Amity

Temple, fr 88 Liberty, S. to Thames

Tenth av. fr 542 West, N. to Harlem R.
1 West
16 W. 12th
34 W. 13th
49 W. 14th
65 W. 15th
82 W. 16th
99 W. 17th
118 W. 18th
134 W. 19th
149 W. 20th
165 W. 21st
178 W. 22d
197 W. 23d
210 W. 24th
228 W. 25th
244 W. 26th
260 W. 27th
277 W. 28th
293 W. 29th
311 W. 30th
325 W. 31st
339 W. 32d
360 W. 33d
376 W. 34th
390 W. 35th
409 W. 36th
422 W. 37th
438 W. 38th
454 W. 39th
470 W. 40th
490 W. 41st
507 W. 42d
525 W. 43d
539 W. 44th

Thames, fr 111 B'way, W to Greenwich
1 Broadway
3 Temple
12 Trinity pl.
29 Greenwich

Theatre al. fr 19 Ann, N. to Beekman

Third, fr 343 Bowery, E. to E. R.
1 Bowery
38 Second av.
99 First av.
142 Avenue A
201 Avenue B
210 East pl.
260 Avenue C
329 Avenue D
356 Manhattan
369 Lewis
394 Goerck

— Mangin
— Tompkins

Third av. fr 402 Bowery to Harlem R.
- 6th
1 7th
- 8th
17 St. Mark's pl.
25 Stuyvesant
27 9th
41 E. 10th
59 E. 11th
77 E. 12th
95 E. 13th
117 E. 14th
137 E. 15th
157 E. 16th
177 E. 17th
193 E. 18th
211 E. 19th
229 E. 20th
247 E. 21st
267 E. 22d
285 E. 23d
305 E. 24th
321 E. 25th
337 E. 26th
353 E. 27th
369 E. 28th
385 E. 29th
401 E. 30th
423 E. 31st
441 E. 32d
455 E. 33d
473 E. 34th
489 E. 35th
505 E. 36th
521 E. 37th
539 E. 38th
559 E. 39th
577 E. 40th
591 E. 41st
609 E. 42d
629 E. 43d
649 E. 44th
659 E. 45th
674 E. 46th
689 E. 47th
707 E. 48th
725 E. 49th
743 E. 50th
763 E. 51st
783 E. 52d
796 E. 53d
815 E. 54th
834 E. 55th
850 E. 56th
871 E. 57th
900 E. 58th
920 E. 59th
937 E. 60th
954 E. 61st
974 E. 62d
1150 E. 73d
1262 E. 80th
1292 E. 81st
1304 E. 82d
1318 E. 83d
1343 E. 84th
1360 E. 85th
1375 E. 86th
1389 E. 87th
1401 E. 88th
1904 E. 123d
1925 E. 124th
1941 E. 125th
1957 E. 126th
1974 E. 127th
1992 E. 128th
2013 E. 129th
2027 E. 130th

Thirteenth av. fr foot of W. 11th, W. to foot W. 29th

Thomas, fr 126 Church, W. to Hudson
1 Church
27 W. B'way
60 Hudson

Thompson, fr 395 Canal, N. to W. 4th
1 Canal
19 Grand
55 Broome
88 Spring
130 Prince
162 W. Houston
204 Bleecker
236 Amity
250 W. 4th

Tompkins, fr 606 Grand, E. to E. R.
1 Grand
11 Broome
29 Delancey
55 Rivington
81 Stanton

Tompkins m'k't, Third av c 6th

Trinity pl. fr 98 Liberty, S. to Edgar
1 Liberty
3 Cedar
11 Thames
48 Rector
63 Exchange al.
78 Edgar

Tryon row, fr 1 Centre, E. to 36 Chatham

Union ct. fr 53 University pl.

Union m'k't, Columbia c E. Houston

Union pl. fr 156 to 232 Fourth av, and fr 851 to 857 B'way
1 E. 14th
11 E. 15th
31 E. 16th
41 E. 17th
62 E. 18th
71 E. 19th

University pl. fr 31 Waverley pl, N. to E. 14th
1 Waverley pl.
8 8th
21 9th
26 E. 10th
42 W. 11th
55 Union ct.
56 E. 12th
72 E. 13th
81 E. 14th

Vandam, fr 13 Macdougal, W. to Greenwich
1 Macdougal
45 Varick
77 Hudson
99 Greenwich

Vandewater, fr 54 Frankfort, E. to Pearl

Vannest pl. Charles st bet Bleecker and W. 4th

Varick, fr 130 Franklin, N. to Carmine
1 Franklin
11 N. Moore
24 Beach
58 Laight
72 Canal
71 Vestry
80 Grand
92 Watts
108 Broome
122 Dominick
136 Spring
154 Vandam
172 Charlton
188 King
204 W. Houston
208 Downing
225 Clarkson
230 Carmine

Varick pl. Sullivan bet W. Houston and Bleecker

Vesey, fr — B'way, W. to N. R.
1 B'way
30 Church
70 Greenwich
84 Washington
110 West

Vestry, fr 428 Canal, W. to N. R.
1 Canal
2 Varick
25 Hudson
47 Greenwich
57 Washington
67 West

Walker, fr 135 W. B'way, E. to Canal
1 W. B'way
29 Church
69 B'way
77 Cortlandt al.
93 Elm
109 Centre
125 Baxter
126 Canal

Wall, fr 86 B'way, E. to E. R.
1 B'way
7 New
20 Nassau
21 Broad
37 Jauncey ct.
51 William
59 Hanover
75 Pearl
89 Water
103 Front
117 South

Warren, fr 260 B'way, W. to N. R.
1 B'way
33 Church
61 College pl.
91 Greenwich
102 Bishop's la.
109 Washington
127 West

Warren pl. Charles bet Greenwich av. & Waverley pl.

Washington, fr 7 Battery pl, N. to W. 12th
1 Battery pl.
39 Morris
97 Rector
121 Carlisle
131 Albany
145 Cedar
153 Liberty
169 Cortlandt
179 Dey
191 Fulton
205 Vesey
221 Barclay
239 Robinson
255 Murray
271 Warren
285 Chambers
299 Reade
305 Duane
319 Jay
336 Harrison
345 Franklin
364 N. Moore
377 Beach
396 Hubert
411 Laight
424 Vestry
439 Desbrosses
453 Watts
474 Hoboken
477 Canal
495 Spring
533 Charlton
547 King
561 W. Houston
578 Clarkson
797 Leroy
714 Morton
531 Barrow
647 Christopher
664 W. 10th
682 Charles
694 Charles la.
600 Perry
620 W. 11th
729 Bank
753 Bethune
765 W. 12th
781 Jane
800 Horatio
814 Gansevoort
— W. 12th

Washington m'k't, Fulton c West

Washington pl. fr 713 B'way, W. to Wooster
1 B'way
5 Mercer
16 Greene
35 Wooster

Washington sq. E. fr W. 4th, N. to Waverley pl.
1 W. 4th
- Washington pl.
- Waverley pl.

Washington sq. N. Waverley pl, fr 29 to 89

Washington sq. W. Macdougal, fr 143 to 165

Water, fr 43 Whitehall, E. to E. R.
1 Whitehall
5 Moore
23 Broad
42 Coenties sl.
49 Cuyler's al.
73 Old sl.
93 Gouverneur la.
117 Wall
133 Pine
139 Depeyster
153 Maiden la.
159 Fletcher
179 Burling sl.
199 Fulton
219 Beekman
251 Peck sl.
279 Dover
322 Roosevelt
361 James sl.
378 Oliver
387 Catharine sl.
431 Market
470 Pike
514 Rutgers
535 Jefferson
565 Clinton
595 Montgomery
613 Gouverneur sl.
620 Gouverneur st.
630 Scammel
684 Jackson
732 Corlears
755 East

Watts, fr 46 Sullivan, W. to N. R.
1 Sullivan
27 Varick
59 Hudson
61 Canal
75 Greenwich
86 Washington
103 West

Waverley pl. fr 727 B'way, W. & N. to Bank
1 B'way
8 Mercer
20 Greene
31 University pl.
36 Wash'n sq. E.
57 Fifth av.
91 Macdougal
128 Sixth av.
141 Gay
168 Grove
170 Christopher
184 W. 10th
171 Charles
179 Perry
181 W. 11th
195 Bank

Weehawken, fr 306 W. 10th, S. to Christopher

Wesley pl. Mulberry, fr E. Houston to Bleecker

West, fr 12 Battery pl, N. to Tenth av.
1 Battery pl.
23 Morris
56 Rector
79 Carlisle
86 Albany
93 Cedar
102 Liberty
113 Cortlandt
122 Dey
130 Fulton
139 Vesey
147 Barclay
159 Robinson
167 Murray
176 Warren
185 Chambers
186 Reade
189 Duane
197 Jay
206 Harrison
213 Franklin
224 N. Moore
234 Beach
247 Hubert
256 Laight
263 Vestry
271 Desbrosses
280 Watts
292 Hoboken
— Canal
303 Spring
320 Charlton
331 King
342 W. Houston
352 Clarkson
361 Leroy
368 Morton
382 Barrow
387 Christopher
395 W. 10th
404 Charles
408 Charles la.

415 Perry
425 W. 11th
444 Bank
470 Bethune
487 W. 12th
505 Jane
520 Horatio
534 Gansevoort
542 Tenth av.

W. Broadway, fr 131 Chambers, N. to Canal
1 Chambers
11 Reade
32 Duane
49 Thomas
63 Worth
82 Leonard
97 Franklin
117 White
122 N. Moore
134 Beach
135 Walker
151 Lispenard
164 York
174 Canal

W. B'way pl. Laurens bet Canal & Grand

W. Houston, fr 609 B'way, W. to N. R.
1 B'way
17 Mercer
39 Greene
61 Wooster
83 Laurens
105 Thompson
127 Sullivan
147 Macdougal
176 Hancock
177 Congress
180 Bedford
235 Varick
275 Hudson
311 Greenwich
328 Washington
349 West

W. 4th, fr 696 B'way, W to W. 13th
1 B'way
14 Mercer
40 Greene
52 Wooster
90 Thompson
126 Macdougal
154 Sixth av.
160 Cornelia
176 Jones
192 Barrow
— W. Wash'n pl.
208 Grove
214 Christopher
230 W. 10th
249 Charles
263 Perry
283 W. 11th
299 Bank
319 W 12th
331 Jane
333 Eighth av.
338 Horatio
356 Gansevoort
— W. 13th

W. 10th, fr 32 Fifth av, W to N. R.
1 Fifth av.
101 Sixth av.
111 Patchin pl.
129 Greenwich
155 Waverley pl.
— W. 4th
215 Bleecker
253 Hudson
267 Greenwich
285 Washington
306 Weehawken
— West

W. 11th, fr 801 B'way, W. to Greenwich
1 B'way
33 University pl.
— Fifth av.
137 Sixth av.
203 Greenwich av.
217 Waverley pl.
255 W. 4th
289 Bleecker
303 Hudson
315 Greenwich
349 Washington
— West

W. 12th, fr 60 Fifth av, W. to N. R.
1 Fifth av.
100 Sixth av.
— Seventh av.
230 Greenwich av.
283 West 4th
306 Eighth av.
316 Hudson
328 Greenwich
372 Washington
411 West
— Thirteenth av.

W. 12th, fr Gansevoort, W. to N. R.
1 Gansevoort
4 Ninth av.
40 Washington
— Tenth av.

W. 13th, fr 72 Fifth av, W. to N. R.
1 Fifth av.
100 Sixth av.
201 Seventh av.
253 Greenwich av.
300 Eighth av.
308 W. 4th
343 Hudson
— Gansevoort
401 Ninth av.
502 Tenth av.
— Thirteenth av.

W. 14th, fr 84 5th av, W. to N. R.
1 Fifth av.
100 Sixth av.
200 Seventh av.
300 Eighth av.
357 Hudson
409 Ninth av.
500 Tenth av.
550 Eleventh av.

W. 15th, fr 96 Fifth av, W. to N. R.
1 Fifth av.
101 Sixth av.
201 Seventh av.
304 Eighth av.
400 Ninth av.
500 Tenth av.
— Eleventh av.

W. 16th, fr 108 Fifth av. W. to N. R.
1 Fifth av.
101 Sixth av.
202 Seventh av.
304 Eighth av.
404 Ninth av.
500 Tenth av.
— Eleventh av.
— Twelfth av.
— Thirteenth av.

W. 17th, fr 116 Fifth av, W. to N. R.
1 Fifth av.
61 Sixth av.
131 Seventh av.
201 Eighth av.
261 Ninth av.
323 Tenth av.
— Eleventh av.
— Thirteenth av.

W. 18th, fr 128 Fifth av, W. to N. R.
1 Fifth av.
61 Sixth av.
121 Seventh av.
134 White's pl.
144 W. 18th st. pl.
180 Eighth av.
245 Ninth av.
305 Tenth av.
— Eleventh av.
— Thirteenth av.

W. 18th st. pl. r 144 W. 18th

W. 19th, fr 140 Fifth av, W. to N. R.
1 Fifth av.
100 Sixth av.
200 Seventh av.
300 Eighth av.
400 Ninth av.
501 Tenth av.
— Eleventh av.
— Thirteenth av.

W. 20th, fr 154 Fifth av, W. to N. R.
— Fifth av.
100 Sixth av.
201 Seventh av.
300 Eighth av.
400 Ninth av.
504 Tenth av

600 Eleventh av.
— Thirteenth av.

W. 21st, fr 160 Fifth av, W. to N. R.
3 Fifth av.
100 Sixth av.
200 Seventh av.
300 Eighth av.
401 Ninth av.
501 Tenth av.
— Eleventh av.
— Thirteenth av.

W. 22d, fr 170 Fifth av, W. to N. R.
1 Fifth av.
100 Sixth av.
201 Seventh av.
300 Eighth av.
400 Ninth av.
504 Tenth av.
— Eleventh av.
— Thirteenth av.

W. 23d, fr 186 Fifth av, W. to N. R.
1 Fifth av.
108 Sixth av.
200 Seventh av.
300 Eighth av.
400 Ninth av.
501 Tenth av.
— Eleventh av.
— Thirteenth av.

W. 24th, fr 1101 B'way, W. to N. R.
1 Broadway
100 Sixth av.
200 Seventh av.
300 Eighth av.
400 Ninth av.
500 Tenth av.
— Eleventh av.
— Thirteenth av.

W. 25th, fr 202 Fifth av, W. to N. R.
1 Fifth av.
7 Broadway
100 Sixth av.
200 Seventh av.
300 Eighth av.
401 Ninth av.
502 Tenth av.
— Eleventh av.
— Thirteenth av.

W. 26th, fr 214 Fifth av, W. to N. R.
1 Fifth av.
11 Broadway
100 Sixth av.
200 Seventh av.
300 Eighth av.
400 Ninth av.
500 Tenth av.
— Eleventh av.

W. 27th, fr 232 Fifth av, W. to N. R.
1 Fifth av.
— Broadway
100 Sixth av.
200 Seventh av.
300 Eighth av.
400 Ninth av.
500 Tenth av.
— Eleventh av.
— Thirteenth av.

W. 28th, fr 248 Fifth av, W. to N. R.
1 Fifth av.
— Broadway
100 Sixth av.
200 Seventh av.
300 Eighth av.
400 Ninth av.
500 Tenth av.
601 Eleventh av.

W. 29th, fr 264 Fifth av, W. to N. R.
1 Fifth av.
28 Broadway
100 Sixth av.
201 Seventh av.
300 Eighth av.
401 Ninth av.
500 Tenth av.
601 Eleventh av.
— Thirteenth av.

W. 30th, fr 280 Fifth av, W. to N. R.
1 Fifth av.
34 Broadway
100 Sixth av
200 Seventh av.
300 Eighth av.
400 Ninth av.
500 Tenth av.
600 Eleventh av.

W. 31st, fr 298 Fifth av, W. to N. R.
1 Fifth av.
49 Broadway
100 Sixth av.
200 Seventh av.
300 Eighth av.
400 Ninth av.
501 Tenth av.
— Eleventh av.
—Twelfth av.

W. 32d, fr 316 Fifth av, W. to N. R.
2 Fifth av.
54 Broadway
100 Sixth av.
202 Seventh av.
301 Eighth av.
401 Ninth av.
500 Tenth av.
— Eleventh av.
— Twelfth av.

W. 33d, fr 330 Fifth av, W. to N. R.
1 Fifth av.
64 Broadway
100 Sixth av.
200 Seventh av.
300 Eighth av.
400 Ninth av.
500 Tenth av.
— Eleventh av.
— Twelfth av.

W. 34th, fr 350 Fifth av, W. to N. R.
1 Fifth av.
101 Sixth av.
107 Broadway
200 Seventh av.
300 Eighth av.
400 Ninth av.
500 Tenth av.
— Eleventh av.
— Twelfth av.

W. 35th, fr 370 Fifth av, W. to N. R.
1 Fifth av.
75 Sixth av.
107 Broadway
168 Seventh av.
268 Eighth av.
371 Ninth av.
459 Tenth av.
523 Eleventh av.

W. 36th, fr 388 Fifth av, W. to N. R.
1 Fifth av.
101 Sixth av.
115 Broadway
201 Seventh av.
301 Eighth av.
400 Ninth av.
501 Tenth av.
— Eleventh av.

W. 37th, fr 406 Fifth av, W. to N. R.
1 Fifth av.
100 Sixth av.
122 Broadway
200 Seventh av.
300 Eighth av.
401 Ninth av.
501 Tenth av.
601 Eleventh av.

W. 38th, fr 420 Fifth av, W. to N. R.
1 Fifth av.
100 Sixth av.
129 Broadway
200 Seventh av.
301 Eighth av.
400 Ninth av.
500 Tenth av.
600 Eleventh av.
— Twelfth av.

W. 39th, fr 438 Fifth av, W. to N. R.
1 Fifth av.
69 Sixth av.
100 Broadway
110 Seventh av.
180 Eighth av.
356 Ninth av.
394 Tenth av.
— Eleventh av.

W. 40th, fr 454 Fifth av, W. to N. R.

1 Fifth av.
100 Sixth av.
134 Broadway
200 Seventh av.
300 Eighth av.
400 Ninth av.
501 Tenth av.
601 Eleventh av.
700 Twelfth av.

W. 41st, fr 717 Sixth av, W. to N. R.
100 Sixth av.
150 Broadway
200 Seventh av.
300 Eighth av.
400 Ninth av.
500 Tenth av.
600 Eleventh av.
700 Twelfth av.

W. 42d, fr Fifth av, W. to N. R.
1 Fifth av.
101 Sixth av.
— Broadway
200 Seventh av.
300 Eighth av.
400 Ninth av.
500 Tenth av.
600 Eleventh av.
700 Twelfth av.

W. 43d, fr Fifth av, W. to N. R.
1 Fifth av.
100 Sixth av.
155 Broadway
200 Seventh av.
301 Eighth av.
400 Ninth av.
501 Tenth av.
601 Eleventh av.
700 Twelfth av.

W. 44th, fr Fifth av, W. to N. R.
1 Fifth av
100 Sixth av.
— Broadway
200 Seventh av.
300 Eighth av.
400 Ninth av.
500 Tenth av.
600 Eleventh av.

W. 45th, fr Fifth av, W. to N. R.
1 Fifth av.
100 Sixth av.
177 Seventh av.
201 B'way
300 Eighth av.
400 Ninth av.
500 Tenth av.
600 Eleventh av.

W. 46th, fr Fifth av, W. to N. R.
1 Fifth av.
100 Sixth av.
162 Seventh av.
200 B'way
300 Eighth av.
400 Ninth av.
501 Tenth av.
600 Eleventh av.

W. 47th, fr Fifth av, W. to N. R.
1 Fifth av.
101 Sixth av.
201 Seventh av.
203 B'way
301 Eighth av.
400 Ninth av.
500 Tenth av.
600 Eleventh av.
— Twelfth av.

W. 48th, fr Fifth av, W. to N. R.
1 Fifth av.
100 Sixth av.
171 Seventh av.
200 B'way
300 Eighth av.
400 Ninth av.
— Tenth av.
600 Eleventh av.

W. 49th, fr Fifth av, W. to N. R.
1 Fifth av.
101 Sixth av.
200 Seventh av.
210 B'way
300 Eighth av.
400 Ninth av.
500 Tenth av.
600 Eleventh av.
700 Twelfth av.

W. 50th, fr Fifth av, W. to N. R.
1 Fifth av.
- Sixth av.
12 Seventh av.
135 B'way
180 Eighth av.
254 Ninth av.
— Tenth av.
— Eleventh av.

W. 51st, fr Fifth av, W. to N. R.
1 Fifth av.
— Sixth av.
— Seventh av.
— Eighth av.
250 Ninth av.
311 Tenth av.
395 Eleventh av.

W. 52d, fr Fifth av, W. to N. R.
1 Fifth av.
100 Sixth av.
200 Seventh av.
— B'way
301 Eighth av.
401 Ninth av.
500 Tenth av.
600 Eleventh av.

W. 53d, fr Fifth av, W. to N. R.
1 Fifth av.
— Sixth av.
— Seventh av.
111 B'way
149 Eighth av.
— Ninth av.
— Tenth av.
— Eleventh av.

W. 54th, fr Fifth av, W. to N. R.
1 Fifth av.
100 Sixth av.
200 Seventh av.
222 B'way
300 Eighth av.
400 Ninth av.
500 Tenth av.
600 Eleventh av.

W. Gotham pl. fr 34 Cherry

W. Washington pl. fr 155 Macdougal, W. to Grove
1 Macdougal
31 Sixth av.
59 Barrow
72 Grove

White, fr 119 W. B'way, E. to Baxter
1 W. B'way
33 Church
57 Franklin al.
68 B'way
77 Cortlandt al.
95 Elm
114 Centre
131 Baxter

White's pl. f 134 W. 18th

Whitehall, f 1 B'way, S. to E. R.
1 Marketfield
2 Bowling gr. row
13 Stone
25 Bridge
32 Pearl
43 Water
48 State
49 Front
64 South

Willett, fr 484 Grand, N. to E. Houston
1 Grand
18 Broome
43 Delancey
71 Rivington
105 Stanton
133 E. Houston

William, fr 67 Stone, N. E. to Pearl
1 Stone
2 Pearl
7 S. William
6 Beaver
35 Exchange pl.
43 Wall
53 Pine
63 Cedar
77 Liberty
83 Maiden la.

92 Platt
106 John
141 Fulton
154 Ann
168 Beekman
180 Spruce
198 Frankfort
207 N. William
239 Duane
249 **New Chambers**
291 **Pearl**

Willow ter. E. 73d n Third av.

Winthrop pl. Greene bet Waverley pl & Clinton pl.

Wooster, fr 355 Canal, N. to W. 4th
1 Canal
28 Grand
55 Broome
92 Spring
128 Prince
166 W. Houston
187 Bleecker
216 Amity pl.
231 Amity
247 W. 4th

Worth, fr 72 Hudson, E. to Baxter
1 Hudson
33 W. B'way
63 Church
— B'way
115 Elm
135 Centre
147 Mission pl.
168 Baxter

York, fr 9 St John's la, E. to W. B'way

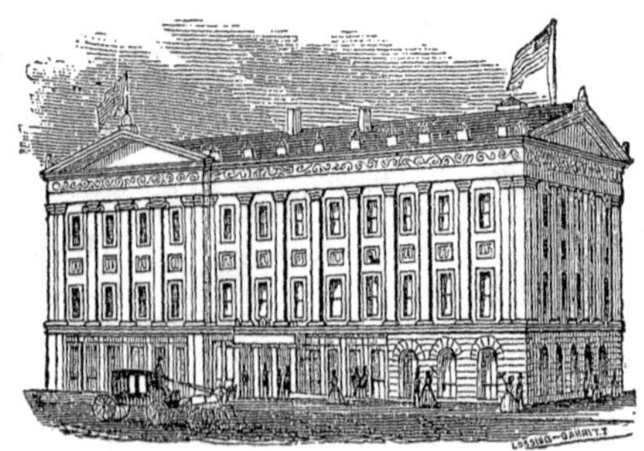

Mercantile Library Building,
Astor Place.

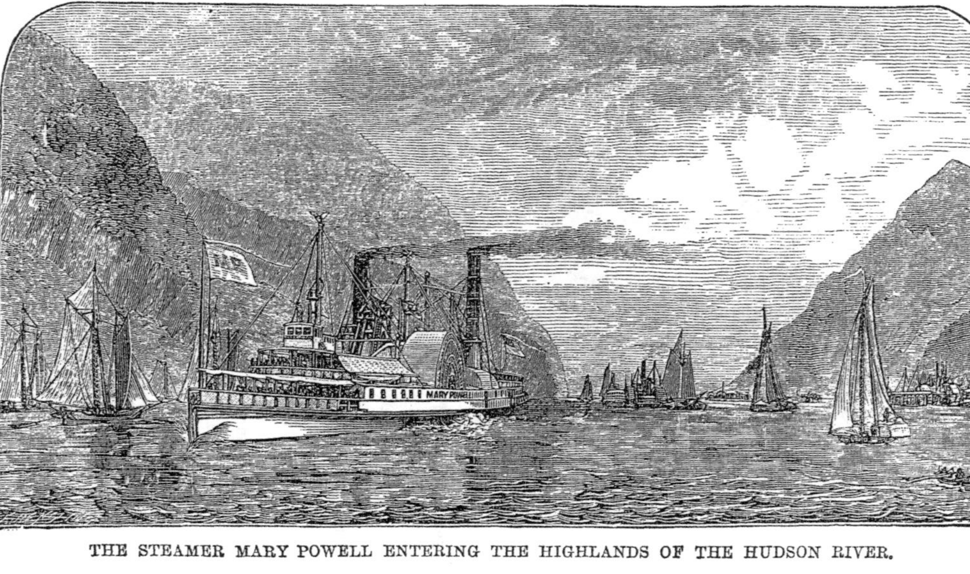

THE STEAMER MARY POWELL ENTERING THE HIGHLANDS OF THE HUDSON RIVER.

CLARENDON HOTEL, Saratoga Springs, N. Y. Charles E. Leland, *Proprietor*.
Also Proprietor of the famous *Delavan Hotel* of Albany and the new and elegant *Rossmore Hotel*, Broadway, 42d Street and Seventh Avenue, New York City. Prices, $4.00 per day.

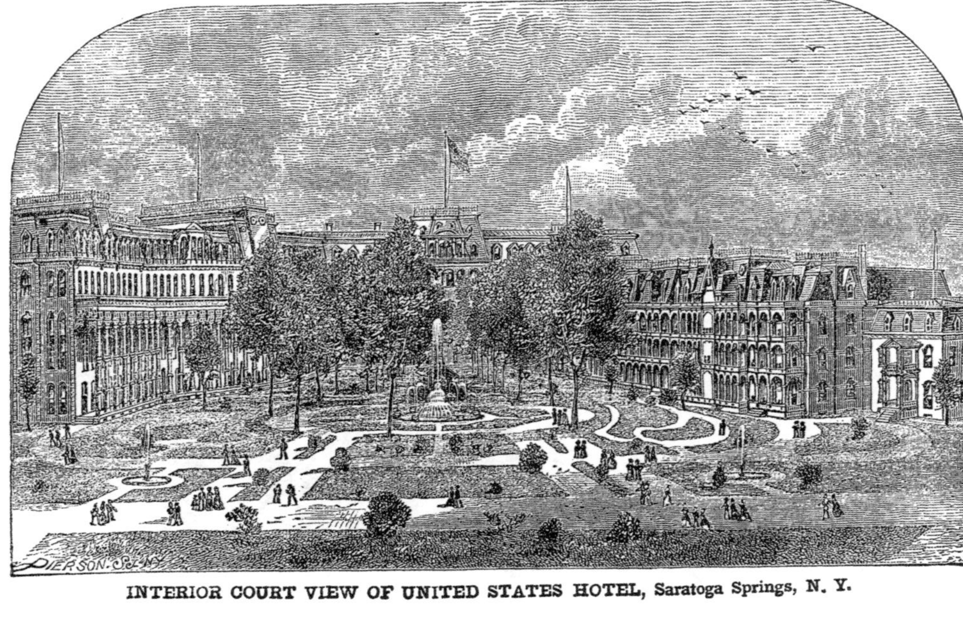

INTERIOR COURT VIEW OF UNITED STATES HOTEL, Saratoga Springs, N. Y.

THE

PALISADE MOUNTAIN HOUSE,

One of the finest summer hotels in the world, is situated on the Lydecker Point of the Palisades of the Hudson River, at Englewood, N. J., opposite Spuyten Duyvil. It is reached by Northern R.R. of N. J. of W. 23d St., or Chambers St., or Steamboats Adelphi and Alexis from foot of Harrison Street, New York. The situation is the most beautiful of any suburban hotel around New York City. The Palisades are four hundred feet or over above the level of the Ocean, and on one of their highest and most prominent outlooks stands the Mountain House. At its foot the Hudson washes the base of the cliffs on which it is built. To the north, bold sweeps of coast, marked with woody headlands and capped with a luxuriant forest, stretch away into the dim distance. Southerly, the spires of the city, the green hills of Staten Island, and the gleam of the Narrows fill the horizon; in front, a superb expanse of hill and dale, river, bay, and Sound spreads itself for miles and miles to the east; while from the upper windows the western view embraces all that beautiful country between the valley of the Overpeck and the Orange Mountains. The air is exceedingly clear and salubrious, and has proved extremely beneficial to invalids and children of delicate constitutions. The hotel is supplied with water from a clear, cool, and delicious spring in the forest, a mile to the westward. The pleasant and various ways of access make it a most desirable summer resort, particularly for gentlemen doing business in the city. The drives are exceeding beautiful, and extend for miles along the Hudson, affording entrancing views of the noble river and charming villas along its banks. The house can accommodate about five hundred guests. The rooms are large, *en suite*, completely, richly, and tastefully furnished. The proprietor, Mr. D. S. Hammond, thoroughly understands his business, and nothing is left undone that could please the most exacting guest. The *cuisine* of the house is equal to any in the country. The grounds about the house are picturesque, the walks charming, and the river convenient for yachting and boating. Gas, hot and cold water, and new bath houses are provided, by which all the advantages of the salt water are made available. An excellent billiard-room and bowling-alley, a fine band of music, and a well-managed livery stable provide every comfort and recreation that could be expected. The fact that the first guests of the Mountain House continue to be its steadfast patrons, year after year, speaks for its special merits and healthfulness more plainly than many words. Among the attractions of Englewood, particularly for families, is the fine Collegiate Institute of the Rev. T. G. Wall, for young ladies and children, and the Englewood Classical and Mathematical School for boys.

PALISADES MOUNTAIN HOUSE, ENGLEWOOD, N. J.

LEXINGTON

CENTRAL STORAGE WAREHOUSE,

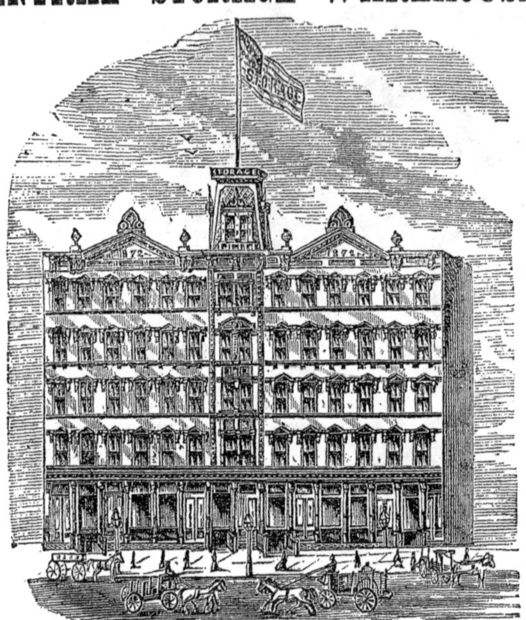

109, 111, 113 & 115 EAST 44th STREET, NEW YORK,

EAST OF THE GRAND CENTRAL DEPOT.

Large, elegant, very desirable and perfect Warehouses for the Storage and Safe-keeping of Furniture, Articles of Value, Works of Art, Baggage, Merchandise, &c., at the most reasonable rates.

The Warehouses, being in the immediate vicinity of "The Grand Central Depot," are convenient for parties out of town, and goods or baggage can be consigned direct to our Warehouses, or we will take charge of them at the depot on receiving letters of instruction, &c.

Goods, packages, &c., taken charge of at the Port of New York, and forwarded upon receipt of Bills of Lading, Invoices, Letters of Instruction, &c., to any place in this Country or Europe as directed. Charges for Freight, Insurance, &c., advanced. Warehouse receipts given on receipt of goods, and delivered to persons authorized to receive them.

A large Carriage Elevator conveys carriages and loaded trucks to upper floors of building without unloading. Watchmen at all times on the premises. Goods taken on Storage day or night. Ladies and Gentlemen are invited to call and examine our Warehouses before making arrangements for Storage elsewhere.

CORNELIUS O'REILLY & BROS,, Proprietors and Owners of Buildings.

COZZENS' HOTEL.—*Cozzens' Landing, West Point, N. Y.*

GOODSELL BROTHERS, *Proprietors.*

This elegant and favorite summer resort stands on a commanding eminence on the west side of the Hudson, 250 feet above the river, and about one mile and a half south of the Military Academy of West Point. It commands one of the finest views on the Hudson, embracing the very heart of the Highlands, and the wildest and most picturesque scenery on this famous river. Its location is remarkably healthful; no cases of sickness having originated at this resort in twenty-five years. West Point was selected as the site of the Military Academy partly because of the healthfulness of the locality. Its location is particularly convenient for New York families, as it is but fifty miles distant, and gentlemen are enabled to visit New York daily, returning to Cozzens' at night if they desire. Among the many places of interest around Cozzens' are the U. S. Military Academy, where daily military exercises of interest occur, old Fort Putnam, Beverly Dock, Robinson House, Buttermilk Falls, etc. The drives among the historic Highlands are celebrated for their enchanting beauty, and one or two, including the five-mile drive to Crystal Lake, have recently been laid out. Distinguished visitors, including our national officials and celebrities, annually visit West Point Academy during the examinations, which begin on the 1st of June.

The hotel is built of brick, and is so constructed that all its rooms command delightful views of the river and mountain scenery. It will accommodate about 400 guests, who are the most refined and respected classes of our metropolitan society. The house is kept in a style to suit such patronage, and Cozzens' Hotel stands unrivaled among our summer resorts in its quiet elegance and comfort.

The table is not surpassed by any hotel in America in luxuries or style, and excellent music daily enlivens the enjoyments of this elegant and unexceptional resort. It can be reached by the Hudson River Railway to Garrison's Station, whence a steam-ferry conveys passengers to Cozzens' Dock; or by Day Line Steamers to West Point, with omnibus to Cozzens' Hotel, or the Mary Powell and Jas. W. Baldwin to Cozzens'. Carriages await at Cozzens' Dock and West Point the arrival of all boats and trains. Daily excursions may be made from New York, stopping for dinner and spending three or four hours at the hotel, returning to the city the same day. Passengers should not mistake the West Point or Government Hotel for Cozzens', but drive to *Cozzens' Hotel*, kept by *Goodsell Bros.*

THE

PALISADE MOUNTAIN HOUSE,

One of the finest summer hotels in the world, is situated on the Lydecker Point of the Palisades of the Hudson River, at Englewood, N. J., opposite Spuyten Duyvil. It is reached by Northern R.R. of N. J. of W. 23d St., or Chambers St., or Steamboats Adelphi and Alexis from foot of Harrison Street, New York. The situation is the most beautiful of any suburban hotel around New York City. The Palisades are four hundred feet or over above the level of the Ocean, and on one of their highest and most prominent outlooks stands the Mountain House. At its foot the Hudson washes the base of the cliffs on which it is built. To the north, bold sweeps of coast, marked with woody headlands and capped with a luxuriant forest, stretch away into the dim distance. Southerly, the spires of the city, the green hills of Staten Island, and the gleam of the Narrows fill the horizon; in front, a superb expanse of hill and dale, river, bay, and Sound spreads itself for miles and miles to the east; while from the upper windows the western view embraces all that beautiful country between the valley of the Overpeck and the Orange Mountains. The air is exceedingly clear and salubrious, and has proved extremely beneficial to invalids and children of delicate constitutions. The hotel is supplied with water from a clear, cool, and delicious spring in the forest, a mile to the westward. The pleasant and various ways of access make it a most desirable summer resort, particularly for gentlemen doing business in the city. The drives are exceeding beautiful, and extend for miles along the Hudson, affording entrancing views of the noble river and charming villas along its banks. The house can accommodate about five hundred guests. The rooms are large, *en suite*, completely, richly, and tastefully furnished. The proprietor, Mr. D. S. Hammond, thoroughly understands his business, and nothing is left undone that could please the most exacting guest. The *cuisine* of the house is equal to any in the country. The grounds about the house are picturesque, the walks charming, and the river convenient for yachting and boating. Gas, hot and cold water, and new bath houses are provided, by which all the advantages of the salt water are made available. An excellent billiard-room and bowling-alley, a fine band of music, and a well-managed livery stable provide every comfort and recreation that could be expected. The fact that the first guests of the Mountain House continue to be its steadfast patrons, year after year, speaks for its special merits and healthfulness more plainly than many words. Among the attractions of Englewood, particularly for families, is the fine Collegiate Institute of the Rev. T. G. Wall, for young ladies and children, and the Englewood Classical and Mathematical School for boys.

PALISADES MOUNTAIN HOUSE, ENGLEWOOD, N. J.
On the Hudson River opposite Spuyten Duyvil.

ROSSMORE HOTEL, Broadway, 42d St. and Seventh Ave., New York, three blocks west of Grand Central Depot, CHARLES E. LELAND, Proprietor. Also Proprietor of the famous *Delavan Hotel* of Albany and the celebrated *Clarendon Hotel* of Saratoga Springs, N. Y. Prices, $4.00 per dav

PIERSON. Sc. N.Y.

ARLINGTON HOTEL,

At WASHINGTON, D. C.

T. ROESSLE & SON, Proprietors.

THE *Arlington Hotel* is well worthy of the first-class patronage which it receives. It is situated on the corner of 15th and H streets, in one of the most interesting portions of the city. The southern wing fronts the beautiful Lafayette Park, in which is the celebrated bronze equestrian statue of Jackson, and opposite which are the "White House," U. S. Treasury Building, and the U. S. War and Navy Departments. The residence of the Secretary of State is a few rods to the north of the hotel—and all the public buildings are within easy distance. The hotel is five stories high, with brown stone front, and is furnished in elegant style, and supplied with a fine passenger elevator—closets on all the floors, signal bells, etc. The dining hall is one of the handsomest and most pleasantly situated in Washington. A large number of the rooms are arranged in suites, with all the conveniences for family use. The proprietors of the Arlington, also conduct the magnificent *Fort William Henry Hotel at Lake George*, the finest summer resort in America. To the patrons of the *Fort William Henry* we need only say that what *it* is in the *summer resort* world the *Arlington* is among the hotels of the Capital.

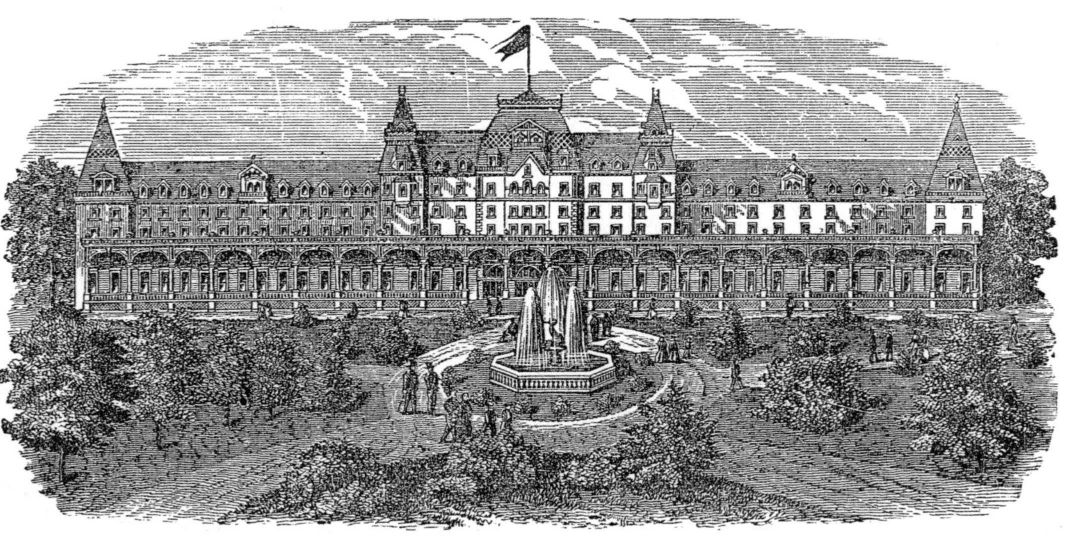

Fort William Henry Hotel.

T. ROESSLE & SON, Proprietors. LAKE GEORGE, CALDWELL. N. Y

ALBANY AND NEW YORK

DAY LINE

ON THE HUDSON RIVER.

Summer Arrangement for Pleasure Travel.

THE STEAMBOATS

C. VIBBARD AND DANIEL DREW

LEAVE NEW YORK DAILY

(SUNDAYS EXCEPTED).

GOING NORTH.	
NEW YORK:	A.M.
Vestry Street	8.10
W. 24th Street	8.30
Nyack and Tarrytown, By Ferryboat	9.55
West Point	11.15
Newburgh	11.50
	P.M.
Poughkeepsie	12.40
Rhinebeck	1.35
Catskill	2.55
Hudson	3.15
ALBANY	5.40

GOING SOUTH.	
	A.M.
ALBANY	8.30
Hudson	10.40
Catskill	11.00
	P.M.
Rhinebeck	12.20
Poughkeepsie	1.15
Newburgh	2 10
West Point	2.40
Nyack and Tarrytown, By Ferryboat	4.05
NEW YORK:	
W. 24th Street	5.30
Vestry Street	5.50

CONNECTING AT ALBANY WITH ALL POINTS NORTH AND WEST.

☞ TRIP TICKETS from New York to West Point and Newburgh, returning same day, $1.00.

TICKETS or COUPONS good on Hudson River Railroad are received on board for passage.

MEALS CAN BE HAD ON THE BOATS.

Leave Albany at 8:30 A.M. on arrival of Chicago Express, on the New York Central Railroad.

ISAAC L. WELSH, G. T. A., New York.

On your way to the Centennial, stop in New York and have your Photograph taken by ABM. BOGARDUS, the Art Photographer of thirty years' experience. Every man, woman and child should have some of my exquisite pictures to show how you looked in the Centennial Year of American Independence. Remember my Gallery is 872 Broadway, cor. of 18th Street, only. No connection with other Galleries carried on by persons pretending to be my successors. Block below and opposite Arnold, Constable & Co's.

It Saves Time,

Labor,

Leather,

Money.

Life Insurance an Element of Success.

THE successful man makes the most of every advantage which nature and circumstance have placed within his reach. He carefully considers his mental abilities and inclinations, and pursues that course for which reason tells him that he is best fitted. The circumstances of his birth and education as well as his physical condition and bodily powers go to influence his pursuits. Every circumstance is then embraced to further his plans. His mind is called upon to assist him to the extent of its forces, and his body should likewise contribute its share to the general fund.

The man who is so fortunate as to possess a sound mind in a sound body, and who desires to make the most of both, cannot consistently neglect the advantages which Life Insurance offers to him. His neighbor may have the elements of success in an equal degree, but some weakness, perhaps unnoticed before, debars him from Life Insurance. The gift of health should thus form an important element in the working capital of him who possesses it, and the taking advantage of the superiority which its possession for the time being gives may be the turning point of success. A Life Policy taken in health and prosperity may be just the security needed in financial troubles, and certainly will be when health is gone and Life Insurance can no longer be obtained.

In choosing a company, that one should be selected which is most careful in the selection of its members, that good health may receive the greatest possible benefits. ***The Phœnix Mutual Life Insurance Company of Hartford, Conn.,*** issues policies on none but the best of risks. It has had 25 years of successful experience, and has assets of the most unquestionable character, of over $10,000,000, invested for the security of its policy-holders. Its business is conducted with economy and prudence, and its members receive the benefits arising from a conservative management to their fullest extent.

AARON C. GOODMAN, *President.*

JONATHAN B. BUNCE, *Vice-Pres.* JOHN M. HOLCOMBE, *Sec'y.*

www.ingramcontent.com/pod-product-compliance
Lightning Source LLC
LaVergne TN
LVHW011223110826
845150LV00006B/1527

* 9 7 8 1 4 2 5 5 1 5 6 3 8 *